THE MYSTIC VISION IN THE GRAIL LEGEND AND IN THE DIVINE COMEDY

¶ Ao Alexādro. vj. Cōtirmatū ꝺotatūqȝ. vij. annoꝝ indulgñ.
Raymundus legat². L. ꝺies. Titus epiſcopus Bäbergeñ cū
ſuo Suffraganeo. lxxx. ꝺies. Cū cōplurib⁹ alijs

Frontispiece of the *Rosarium Celestis curiæ et patriæ triumphalis,* Jacob
Locher, Nuremburg, 1517. From *Renaissance und Humanismus,* Ludwig
Geiger, 1882.

THE MYSTIC VISION IN THE GRAIL LEGEND AND IN THE DIVINE COMEDY

BY

LIZETTE ANDREWS FISHER, Ph.D.

AMS PRESS, INC.
NEW YORK
1966

Manufactured in the United States of America

This Monograph has been approved by the Department of English and Comparative Literature in Columbia University as a contribution to knowledge worthy of publication.

A. H. THORNDIKE,
Executive Officer

PREFACE

THE addition of even a single page to the voluminous criticism of the *Grail Legend* and the *Divine Comedy* can be justified only by the hope of suggesting a fresh interpretation in the light of hitherto unnoticed facts. But they have been examined from so many different points of view that it would seem impossible to find any line of thought explanatory of questions in either, much less one which clears up problems in both.

Nevertheless such a line of thought is, I believe, to be found in the history of the doctrine of transubstantiation, which from the controversies of the ninth century to its culmination in the Lateran Council of 1215 seems, strangely enough, to have received little attention from the standpoint of its literary influence, though it needs but a moment's reflection to perceive that a dogma so closely connected with the life and thought of the later Middle Ages must have affected contemporary literature. Emphasis on the sacramental system of the church as its great agent of salvation, and the special glorification of the eucharist as chief among sacraments, received authoritative recognition in the decree of this council, which declared transubstantiation an article of faith, and placed it at the beginning of its confession in immediate connection with the fundamental doctrines of the Trinity and the Incarnation. While the religious fervor thus evidenced found outward expression in elaboration of eucharistic ritual and in the feast of Corpus Christi, its spiritual influence is no less marked in the mysticism of the day.

The eucharist was one means, and not the least important, by which man might achieve union with God. Through it the soul entered into union with God Incarnate, His splendor being sacramentally veiled in mercy to finite powers, and the intuitive knowledge of transubstantiation, conceived as the miracle whereby the special presence of God was invoked, was claimed as a part, at least, of the mystic vision.

Though it is manifestly impossible that so stupendous a belief could have been without its effect on contemporary literature, it was not from the doctrinal point of view that this study had its beginning, but rather from a desire to understand certain unexplained features of the closing cantos of the *Purgatory*. The point of departure was the cry of greeting to Beatrice as she appears in the Earthly Paradise, *Benedictus qui venis*, words which not only hailed the entry of Christ into Jerusalem but which day by day in the mass herald the expected coming of Christ to the altar at the moment of consecration. Dante, fully aware of the eucharistic association with the words, must have been conscious that by their use at this point he was suggesting an allegorical connection between the coming of Beatrice and the sacramental coming of Christ. Such an allegory, with all its ceremonial detail, is not only entirely consistent with the belief and worship familiar to Dante, but leads also to a genuinely organic interpretation of the whole episode. Just as the eucharistic presence of Christ vouchsafed to the church is foretaste and pledge of the final vision of God, so the revelation of Beatrice in the Earthly Paradise is the foreshadowing of the revelation of God with which the *Divine Comedy* closes.

The application of the theory to the Grail legend came about, almost accidentally, through the questions which arise in regard to those glimpses of the Earthly Paradise which appear now and again in its background. That the influence of the dogma of transubstantiation might offer an explana-

tion of the knottiest point of the whole Grail problem, that
of the fusion of the Celtic story of the Quest and the Christian legend of Joseph of Arimathea, was at the outset far
from the thought of the writer, who can honestly deny
having fitted facts into a previously conceived theory. On
the contrary, the tendency of all the facts as they were col-
lected and compared to point to one conclusion and to
answer many and diverse questions was viewed at first with
the suspicion always aroused by extraordinarily detailed and
minute correspondence. So many good theories have
snapped when stretched to cover too many points!

This study is offered for the consideration of those who
are interested in the question of the meaning of literature
to those for whom it was created, in this case a medieval
audience unconscious of "sources" but greatly liking an
implied moral. Though the present work is an investigation into the influence of eucharistic teaching and practice
in a circumscribed field, there are undoubtedly other literary
questions which may find an answer in the same influence
and which may therefore repay study from the same point
of view.

In the matter of acknowledgment and thanks my credi-
tors are many and words a most inadequate repayment.
To Professor J. B. Fletcher, in whose seminar I learned to
value Dante's background of religion and philosophy, my
obligation is not to be measured, and extends beyond public
teaching to private advice and encouragement. To Professor
W. W. Lawrence I owe the enrichment of my own meagre
acquaintance with medieval romance from his ample store.
Both have given endless patient consideration to the work
of criticism and suggestion. To other members of the
department of English and Comparative Literature of Columbia University, notably to Professor A. H. Thorndike,
I am grateful for immediate attention to the first presentation of my theory, and for generous and unflagging interest

in its development. This interest has also been shared by many fellow-students, some of whom have given valuable assistance in the correction of proof.

For the books required I am indebted not only to the authorities and staff of the Library of Columbia University, of the New York Public Library, and of the Peabody Library, Baltimore, but also to those of the General and Union Theological Seminaries, New York, for without their special collections such a study could not have been made at all.

I should like also to make special mention of the monumental work of MM. Rohault de Fleury from whose study of the archeology of the mass all the illustrations, except the frontispiece, have been taken.

L. A. F.

COLUMBIA UNIVERSITY,
  December, 1916.

CONTENTS

INTRODUCTION 1

TRANSUBSTANTIATION IN HISTORY, THEOLOGY AND DEVOTION . 7

THE MYSTIC VISION IN THE LEGEND OF THE GRAIL 29

THE MYSTIC VISION IN THE DIVINE COMEDY 85

APPENDICES 117

BIBLIOGRAPHY 139

INDEX 145

INTRODUCTION

THE modern student of history is admittedly more interested in the thoughts than in the deeds of the past. Looking to the former for the explanation of the latter, he grudges no time spent in understanding the mental attitude of a period, in reconstructing it with all possible sympathy for its peculiarities and without any trace of condescension to its limitations. Students of letters have been somewhat slower to realize that literature no less than history must involuntarily reflect contemporary thinking and feeling, but they are now very generally agreed that the background of ideas and sentiment must be reconstructed before we can hope to know what any literature meant to the audience for which it was produced.

In the work of such reconstruction the method employed has been, for the most part, based on the theory of evolution. Ever conscious of the idea of development, students have sought to find the key to all things in their origins rather than in their contemporary associations; in other words, in their heredity rather than in their environment. Scholarly energy has largely been devoted to the study of sources in literature and history as well as in language. In the field of folk lore and popular story scholars have zealously followed every clew and preserved every tale lingering anywhere on the lips of the people, and when we read the carefully arranged results of their labors we are startled to find therein the germs of every story that has ever been told. Investigation of primitive worship, custom, and art has thrown light into many a dark corner of history and letters, and has afforded a clew to more than one tangle.

But, after all, while the antecedents of every vital thing, idea, or person are always interesting and to be reckoned with in acquiring knowledge of it, the great force which moulds it is its own living present. It is a part of all that it has met even more than it is a consequence of its origins.

In the study of literature, the literature of the Middle Ages especially, the importance of the immediate environment has been recognized, and a good deal of recent research has been devoted to geographical and historical setting, to contemporary manners, customs, and superstitions. Much less of zeal and interest has been expended on the study of contemporary theology. The religion of the Middle Ages has too often been dismissed rather curtly with casual mention of "medieval theology" or "monkish notions," and treated as a static, undisputed body of belief, fixed and immutable from the sixth century to the sixteenth. One reason for this is probably that while the average modern man has drifted too far from dogmatic theology to recognize its influence instinctively it is still too close to him to arouse attention and stimulate interest. It would, however, be admitted that no department of human activity remains unchanged throughout the centuries, and that for the thousand years of the Middle Ages the best intellectual capacity and attainment were devoted to questions of God and the soul, and the relation between them. On the answers to these questions and on the dutiful acceptance of them depended man's salvation; that is, his rescue from literal damnation and his ultimate attainment of heaven. By religion alone could he hope to be saved, and religion was entrusted to the church. So all life was viewed through the glass of theology, the church's dogmatic expression of religion, and it is impossible to conceive of anything more closely related to conduct or more likely to be reflected in all forms of literature.

In the religion of the Middle Ages, as indeed in all religion whatsoever, there is the element of mysticism. To use the words "mystic vision" in a title is to involve oneself in an apology at the outset. The word "mystic" has as wide a mantle as charity and covers a multitude of follies if not of sins. Mysticism is only too often a loose term for any spiritual manifestation difficult of explanation, and in consequence is dismissed by many people as synonymous with moonshine. It is applied to everything outside the plainest matter of fact, from Piers Ploughman's vision to the latest fashion in eastern cults. But, as has been well said, a man is not a visionary when he has a vision, but only when he has nothing else, and the genuine mystic is usually a surprisingly direct person, his mysticism, to himself, really a very simple (one wants to say practical) matter. Accepting the proposition that to know God is the chief end and aim of existence, he finds that such knowledge comes to him by other faculties than the rational. It is by intuition that he attains the mystic vision in which he claims to realize absolute truth and to taste absolute blessedness.

This spiritual attitude is peculiar to no age, nationality, nor form of religion. There have always been those who did not even try "by searching to find out God." To them, when ripe for the experience, there came direct, intuitive knowledge of Him. There are, of course, degrees of illumination; souls vary in their capacity to receive light, and an inferior capacity may be increased by means of contemplation and spiritual exercises; but in each degree the mystic vision is the nearest approach to the final vision of God attainable by man while still in the flesh. It is an endowment akin to the artistic gift — that intuitive, uninstructed, unexplainable choice of the true color, the right line, the harmonizing note, the inevitable word:

> God has a few of us whom He whispers in the ear:
> The rest may reason and welcome.

Neo-Platonic ecstasy was such an experience, as was also the *gnosis* of Alexandria. Such, too, is the top rung of the ladder of contemplation and the "inner light" of the followers of George Fox. But always and everywhere it is the foretaste of the fruition of God.

Though the mystic approach to the divine is a spiritual experience, widespread and persistent, its manifestations are as varied as those of every other human experience. Broadly speaking, the mystic is a soul apart; his revelation is direct; a way is opened before him. Those who attempt to follow in his footsteps, lacking the direct light, are misled by wandering fires. There are, however, exceptions to this state of isolation, and one of the best defined is the mystic school of the twelfth and thirteenth centuries.

The school, often called by historians of medieval philosophy that of the scholastic mystics,[1] is remarkable not only because it may be called a school at all, but because its representatives united fervent mystical devotion not only to orthodoxy, but to one of the most rigid of all expressions of it, the scholastic theology consummated in the work of Aquinas. The manifestations of this particular form of mysticism must later be discussed at some length, but at this point we may say that it found one way of attaining its goal, the knowledge of God, in the means of grace afforded by the church, especially in its sacramental system. These scholastic mystics lived at the time when the sacraments of the church were attaining a position of very great importance in theological discussion.

Chief among sacraments is the eucharist, for in it sign and thing signified are one, even Christ, and so by its means man attains on earth to communion with God. Controversies as to the exact nature of Christ's presence in the sacrament of the altar took the place of the controversies over

[1] Cf. W. R. Inge, *Christian Mysticism*, p. 140; M. de Wulf, *History of Medieval Philosophy*, tr. Coffey, p. 215.

the Trinity and the Incarnation which engrossed the early church, and, as a result of these controversies, the eucharist became for the later Middle Ages the focus of all worship as well as the supreme means of grace and of participation in the divine life. Eucharistic devotion colored all ritual and influenced all forms of art. The daily mass was the daily miracle of the presence of God, and was so accepted, in some sense or other, by every christened man, — peasant, priest, or knight. Around it gathered much gross superstition, it is true, but also much artistic expression and poetic fervor.

Mysticism is an attitude of the human spirit, ubiquitous and perpetual, and by the thirteenth century it had adjusted itself to the sacramental system of the church. It was a vital part of human experience, and as such must be reflected in contemporary literature; its omission would require far more explanation than its inclusion. But before we can discuss intelligently specific instances of literary influence we must examine the evidence for the conspicuous importance of eucharistic devotion in the religious life of the time, and trace the development of the doctrine concerning the eucharist chiefly responsible for such importance; the doctrine, namely, of transubstantiation.

TRANSUBSTANTIATION IN HISTORY, THEOLOGY, AND DEVOTION

Se nascens dedit socium,
Convescens in edulium,
Se moriens in pretium,
Se regnans dat in præmium.

O salutaris hostia,
Quæ cœli pandis ostium,
Bella premunt hostilia,
Da robur, fer auxilium.

— THOMAS AQUINAS

TRANSUBSTANTIATION IN HISTORY, THEOLOGY, AND DEVOTION

I

In the month of November, 1215, there assembled in Rome the twelfth ecumenical council, historically known as the Fourth Lateran, but commonly cited in canon law as "the general Council of the Lateran" without further qualification, or again, as "the Great Council." [1] It came together at the call of Innocent III, who had long dreamed of presiding over such a gathering, and it was at once the climax and conclusion of his career — he died a few months later — and the supreme moment of the papacy as an unquestioned authority in European affairs.

Innocent III (Lotario de'Conti di Segni, c. 1160–1216) was of noble birth and educated in the most approved manner of the Middle Ages. After his early training in Rome he went to the university of Paris, where, under Peter of Corbeil, he laid the foundations of his profound knowledge of scholastic philosophy; later, at Bologna, he acquired as thoroughly canon and civil law. He seemed preëminently a scholar, and, though he attained some eminence in church affairs, he did not advance beyond the diaconate, having been created cardinal-deacon by his uncle Clement III. His uncle was succeeded by Celestine III, who belonged to the rival family of the Orsini, so Lotario withdrew from active affairs and devoted himself to study. In his retirement he produced, among other works, six books under the title, *Mysterium evangelicae legis ac sacramenti eucharistiae*, interesting in view of his subsequent official pronouncement

[1] Cf. H. Leclercq, *Cath. Enc.*, Art. *Lateran*.

in regard to eucharistic doctrine. After the death of the Orsini pope he was unanimously elected to the papacy, and, in order to qualify for it, passed through the stages of priest and bishop on successive days. Thus, when less than forty, he found himself qualified by birth, training, and position to assert afresh the papal supremacy claimed by Hildebrand, and by force of character and personality to make the claim a reality.

After most imposing ceremonies of accession, which included a great procession, Innocent turned his attention to the affairs of Rome. He reduced the warring factions to order and induced the populace to forego in his favor its ancient claim to elect the senate. He vested the executive powers of the senate in a single senator, directly or indirectly selected by himself. He found Italy restless and sullen under the imperial rule of Henry VI, and, taking advantage of the strife between rival factions after the early death of that emperor, he cleared the great Italian fiefs of German feudatories, deposed the imperial prefect in Rome itself, and saw to it that his own *rectores* governed the patrimony of St. Peter.[1] So within one year of his election to the papacy he succeeded in putting pope above emperor in Italy, in token whereof he managed to be appointed guardian of the infant son of Henry VI, the future Frederick II.

From this secure standing point he proceeded to make his authority felt all over Europe. His quarrel with England is the best known instance of this assertion of papal rights. There he used interdict and excommunication to support his claim to bestow preferment, enforcing his contention with a high and heavy hand, the weight of which was never forgotten. The English episode is, however, only one among many. He excommunicated Alfonso I of Leon for marrying within the forbidden degrees, and for similar reasons

[1] Cf. Gregorovius, *History of the City of Rome in the Middle Ages,* Bk. IX.

annulled the marriage of the crown prince Alfonso of Portugal. Pedro II of Aragon submitted as the pope's vassal and received coronation at his hand. He was arbiter between two rival claimants to the throne of Norway, and acted in the same capacity in Sweden. He prepared a crusade against the Moors in Spain, and undertook the Fourth Crusade while doing his utmost for the Latinization of the Eastern Empire. As champion of orthodoxy he instituted the crusade of obliteration against the Albigenses. If not the originator of the famous comparison of the spiritual power to the sun and the temporal to the moon, so bitterly discussed by Dante,[1] he was its undaunted champion. His profound knowledge of both civil and canon law furnished him the machinery for his purpose: the driving power came from his sincere belief in theocracy [2] and his own indomitable will and personality. Says Gregorovius, "The spectacle of a man who, if only for the moment, ruled the world according to his will in tranquil majesty is sublime and marvellous." [3]

No greater opportunity to display this majesty can be conceived than that afforded by a General Council, which was for a pope of the Middle Ages what a great feudal gathering was for king or emperor.[4] The pope's imperious summons to christendom was issued more than two years before the actual assembling, and excuses were not well received. Prelates were to come to Rome if possible; but if age or infirmity could be pleaded they were commanded to

[1] *De Monarchia,* III: iv.

[2] To the ambassadors of Philip Augustus he said: "To princes power is given on earth, but to priests it is attributed also in heaven; the former only over bodies, but the latter also over souls. Whence it follows that by so much as the soul is superior to the body, the priesthood is superior to the kingship." — Cit. W. A. Phillips, *Enc. Brit.,* Art. *Innocent III.*

[3] *Op. cit.* Bk. IX: III: i.

[4] Cf. A. Luchaire, *Innocent III et le quatrième concile de Latran, Rev. historique,* XCVII: 225–263.

send responsible representatives under threat of canonical discipline.

The urgency of the summons and the length of time allowed in which to obey it account in part for the vast size of the gathering, perhaps the greatest ecclesiastical assembly the world has ever seen. Over four hundred bishops were in attendance, and many others were represented by high ecclesiastics. Eight hundred abbots and the Latin patriarchs, established in the East by Innocent, appeared. There were also representatives of the Emperor Frederick II, the Latin emperor of Constantinople, the kings of England, France, Aragon, Hungary and Jerusalem. The scene of the council, the Lateran, to Dante "supreme above all mortal things," [1] was a fitting background for the pomp of the gathering.

The three great sessions, about a fortnight apart, were held in the basilica of St. John Lateran. [2] In it a raised throne had been erected for the sovereign pontiff, who, says Richard, "showed himself coming forth as a bridegroom from his chamber, and ascending, took his seat on the tribunal to which centurions and tribunes advanced." [3] A fanfare of trumpets proclaimed silence when the ruler of rulers would speak, a necessary measure, probably, in view of the size of the audience. The crowd at the opening service was

[1]   "quando Laterano
    Alle cose mortali andò di sopra."
                    Paradiso, XXXI: 35, 36.

[2] For details of this council I am indebted to the article by Luchaire to which I have already referred, p. 11. He gives as his chief authority on the council Richard de St. Germano, notary to Frederick II. "Il assista au concile et l'a décrit en témoin qui sait voir et entendre." p. 236.

[3] "Se manifestavit . . . egrediens tamquam sponsus de thalamo suo et ascendens sedit pro tribunali, cui centuriones suberant et tribuni." On this Luchaire comments (p. 240): "Expressions classiques par lesquelles le notaire de Frédéric II, qui a fait ses humanités, désigne sans doute les gardes pontificaux."

so great that it is said one ecclesiastic, the bishop of Amalfi, fell in the press and was trampled to death, and that on another occasion one or more delegates were smothered.

It was, however, at the third session, November 30, that the Pope read the seventy canons which he had prepared. It is generally admitted that there was no discussion and that the council, without more ado, promulgated the canons as matters of faith.[1] In the very first of them the orthodox faith was proclaimed, and for the first time the doctrine of the eucharist was brought into the proceedings of a General Council.[2] After the statement of the great Christian mysteries of the Trinity and Incarnation, the canon proceeded to the assertion that outside the universal church of the faithful none can be saved. In it priest as well as sacrifice is Christ Himself, whose body and blood are contained in that sacrament of the altar under the species of bread and wine, transubstantiated, the bread into the body and the wine into the blood, by divine power, in order that for the completion of the mystery of unity we may ourselves receive of His what He received of ours.[3]

"What is important here," says Harnack, "is that the doctrine of the eucharist is immediately attached to the confession of the Trinity and Incarnation. *In this way it is represented even in the symbol as having a most intimate relation to these doctrines, as, indeed, forming with them a*

[1] "The fathers of the council did little more than approve the seventy decrees presented to them; this approbation, nevertheless, sufficed to impart to the acts thus formulated and promulgated the value of ecumenical decrees." *Cath. Enc.*, Art. *Lateran.*

[2] Cf. *Hastings' Enc.*, Art. *Councils and Synods.*

[3] "Una vero est fidelium universalis ecclesia, extra quam nullus omnino salvatur. In qua idem ipse sacerdos, et sacrificium Jesus Christus; cujus corpus et sanguis in sacramento altaris sub speciebus panis et vini veraciter continentur; transubstantiatis, pane in corpus, et vino in sanguinem, potestate Divina, ut ad perficiendum mysterium unitatis accipiamus ipsi de suo quod accepit ipse de nostro." — *Mansi,* XXII: 982.

unity . . . the real presence obtained the same value as the Trinity and the two-nature doctrine, so that every one was regarded as an ecclesiastical anarchist who called it in question." Harnack goes on to say that "the novelty in the symbol — the direct attachment of the eucharist dogma to the Trinity and Christology — is the most distinctive and boldest act of the Middle Ages. Compared with this immense innovation the addition of the 'filioque' weighs very lightly." [1]

The doctrine of transubstantiation was thus explicitly and finally established as the orthodox belief of all Christian men, and to deny it was to read oneself out of the church militant and triumphant. Innocent had not only demonstrated the authority he had asserted, but had secured an immense backing for the points of doctrine and discipline which he wished to emphasize.[2] Richard says it was in honor of the Trinity that the pope completed the council on the third day,[3] but whatever the motive, the great pope, using as a mouthpiece the greatest ecclesiastical assembly the world has ever seen, took three days to end the controversies of three centuries, and to declare definitely and authoritatively the consecrated host identical with Christ, and so the cornerstone of the church.[4]

[1] A. Harnack, *History of Dogma*, VI: 53 ff.

[2] Cf. Luchaire, *op. cit.* 227. "L'assemblée européenne de 1215 a été le signe visible, éclatant, de la suprématie spirituelle et temporelle conquise sur le monde par la monarchie romaine, telle que l'avait faite Innocent III. Mais il y a autre chose. Le programme de concile comportait des résolutions à prendre d'une tellê importance qu'il fallait que l'universalité des fidèles fût là pour donner les sanctions nécessaires."

[3] "Sicque propter causam Trinitatis pontifex sanctam synodum trina sezione complevit." — Cit. Luchaire, page 241.

[4] "If there was one doctrine upon which the supremacy of the medieval church rested, it was the doctrine of transubstantiation. It was by his exclusive right to the performance of the miracle which was wrought in the mass that the lowliest priest was raised high above princes." — J. R. Green, *History of the English People*, Bk. IV: iv.

II

Considering that the "breaking of bread" with "prayers" [1]
was from the beginning the central act of Christian worship and privilege of initiation, it is not surprising that discussion as to the nature of Christ's presence in the eucharist
and the means whereby it is effected should give rise to controversy, and if the records of the controversies themselves
are voluminous, comment on the controversies is literally
interminable. We are here concerned chiefly with the disputes arising in the middle of the ninth century, which
continued, with more or less intermittent fervor, until their
official and triumphant settlement at the Great Council.
Any outline of them must condense scores of years and
volumes of argument into sentences, but it is worth while
to make the attempt to gain an idea of the clash of opinion
which was effectively ended in 1215, only to be renewed by
the teaching of Wyclif.

In the ninth century Paschasius, a monk of Corbey,
maintained that in the eucharist the bread is converted into
the very body of Christ. Ratramnus of the same abbey
defended the opinion that there is no conversion of the bread
and that though the body of Christ is present, it is in a
spiritual way. "Scotus Erigena had supported the view that
the sacraments of the altar are figures of the body of Christ;
that they are a memorial of the true body and blood of
Christ." [2] But it was only in the eleventh century that the
whole matter attained a very fury of controversy as a consequence of the teaching of Berengarius, director of the
Cathedral School at Tours. He adopted the spiritualized
theory of Ratramnus and Scotus, holding that the whole
body of Christ is received by the heart, not by the mouth.[3]

[1] *Acts*, II: 42.

[2] G. M. Sauvage, *Cath. Enc.*, Art. *Berengarius*.

[3] "Christi corpus totum constat accipi ab interiore homine, fidelium corde, non ore."

Berengarius more than once signed retractions only to attack them, and it is difficult to make a clear statement of his teaching. A summary from the Roman Catholic point of view is, therefore, of special value.

"In order to understand his opinion, we must observe that, in philosophy, Berengarius had rationalistic tendencies and was a nominalist. Even in the study of questions of faith, he held that reason is the best guide. Reason, however, is dependent upon and is limited by sense perception. Authority, therefore, is not conclusive; we must reason according to the data of our senses. There is no doubt that Berengarius denied transubstantiation (we mean the substantive conversion expressed by the word; the word was used for the first time by Hildebert of Lavardin); it is not absolutely certain that he denied the real presence, though he certainly held false views concerning it. Is the body of Christ present in the eucharist, and in what manner? On this question the authorities appealed to by Berengarius are, besides Scotus Erigena, St. Jerome, St. Ambrose, and St. Augustine. These fathers taught that the sacrament of the altar is the figure, the sign, the token of the body and blood of the Lord. These terms, in their mind, apply to what is external and sensible in the holy eucharist, and do not, in any way, imply the negation of the real presence of the true body of Christ. (St. Aug. *Serm.* 143, n. 3: Gerbert, *Libellus de Corp. e Sang. Domini*, n. 4. *Migne*, CLXXXIX: 177.) For Berengarius the body and blood of Christ are really present in the holy eucharist; but the presence is an intellectual or spiritual presence. The substance of the bread and the substance of the wine remain unchanged in their nature, but by consecration they become spiritually the very body and blood of Christ. This spiritual body of Christ is the *res sacramenti;* the bread and the wine are the figure, the sign, the token, *sacramentum.*" [1]

---

[1] Sauvage, *op. cit.*

Berengarius made final retraction and died in union with the church in 1088, but the influence of his principles was widespread, for pupils had come to him from all parts of France, and his teaching was attacked by leading theologians, among them Lanfranc, Durandus, and the Benedictines. "The transmutation theory of Paschasius . . . was further developed by the opponents of Berengar.[1] First, the mystery was conceived of still more sensuously, at least by some (*manducatio infidelium*); secondly, there was a beginning, though with caution, to apply to dogma the 'science' that was discredited in the opponent. The crude conceptions (which embraced the *total* conversion) were put aside and an attempt was made to unite the older deliverances of tradition with the new transmutation doctrine, as also to adopt the Augustinian terminology, by means of dialectic distinctions, to the still coarsely realistic view of the subject."[2]

The Roman Catholic view of this development is as follows:

"The error of Berengarius, as is the case with other heresies, was the occasion which favored and even necessitated, a more explicit presentation and a more precise formulation of Catholic doctrine about the holy eucharist. . . . The Council of Rome, in 1079, in its condemnation of Berengarius, expresses more clearly than any document before it the nature of this substantial change. . . . Though the feast of Corpus Christi was officially established only in the thirteenth century, its institution was probably occasioned by these eucharistic controversies. The same may be said of the ceremony of the elevation of the host after the consecration of the holy sacrifice of the mass."[3] And again:

[1] "Yet everything acquired settled form only in the thirteenth century; the questions resulting from the new doctrine are innumerable." Harnack, *op. cit.*, VI: 51n.

[2] Harnack, *op. cit.*, VI: 51.

[3] Sauvage, *op. cit.*

"After the Berengarian controversy the blessed sacrament was in the eleventh and twelfth centuries elevated for the express purpose of repairing by its adoration the blasphemies of heretics and strengthening the imperilled faith of Catholics. In the thirteenth century were introduced for the greater glorification of the Most Holy, the theophoric processions . . . and also the feast of Corpus Christi." [1]

Whether this shift of emphasis and consequent supreme exaltation of the eucharist be viewed as innovation or reparation, there can be no question that in the later Middle Ages the eucharist was viewed not only as the continual extension of the Incarnation and the centre of Christian worship, but was also the supreme expression of all spiritual life and the focus of devotional expression, poetry, and drama.[2]

III

We come now to the relation of this preëminent importance of the eucharist to that mysticism which, *ut semper*,

[1] J. Pohle, *Cath. Enc.*, Art. *Eucharist*.

[2] "Worship and adoration found a striking and noble expression in the medieval mass, and in the prayers contained in some of the popular books of instruction. To the men of the Middle Ages the mass was the mystery *par excellence* of the church. Around it there gathered all the splendor which art and music could provide. . . . The medieval mass kept the memory of the passion of Christ vividly before the minds of the worshippers. The popular books of devotion and the mystical commentators on the mass alike emphasize the conception of the mass as a sacred drama exhibiting and rehearsing again and again the story of the Lord's passion 'until He come.' " — J. H. Shrawley, Hastings' *Enc. of Religion and Ethics*, Art. *Eucharist to End of Middle Ages*.

"In the sacrament of the Supper and the doctrine regarding it, the church gave expression to everything that it highly prized — its dogma, its mystical relation to Christ, the fellowship of believers, the priest, the sacrifice, the miraculous power which God had given to His church, the satisfaction of the sensuous impulse in piety, and so forth." — Harnack, *op. cit.* VI: 233 f.

ubique et ab omnibus, concerns itself with the immediate
contact of the soul with the divine. Varying in its expression with various religions, with various conceptions of the
soul and God, it is always somewhere in the life of man.
Always there are some to whom it is given to experience while
still in the flesh some of the freedom of the released soul, to
realize the love of God and to become one with Him. The
ecstasy of Platonic love takes the soul back to the divine
from which it came; and Philo, Hellenized Jew, found in
contemplation the means of putting the soul into that way
of return, the path of direct, intuitive knowledge of God.
Plotinus, though he developed this contact with God into
coalescence with Him, found material existence an estrange-
ment, and was forced to admit that even for the most expert
these times of union must be brief and occasional. To the
Christian Platonists of Alexandria this direct knowledge, or
gnosis, was above faith, which they regarded as the cut and
dried expression of truth, sufficient for those who, for lack
of direct knowledge, must needs take it at second hand.

It is not specially difficult to see that while in the higher
type of men such theories produce characters of the loftiest
virtue, there are likely to be also exceedingly unlovely
results. The notion of one's own private enlightenment
and law entirely demoralizes the wilful soul, who finds in it
justification for breaking all bounds of ethics and morals,
and so spiritual freedom rapidly degenerates into carnal
license. It is, therefore, not surprising to find the law-
abiding Roman mind distrusting mystic philosophy and
laying stress on the reality of sin and the need of forgiveness:
only by process of repentance and amendment of life is one
entitled to expect union with God. For Augustine the love
of God is not only the means of knowing Him, but the motive
of obedience to His laws. The rare moments in which man,
losing himself, finds God, whose fruition is the essence of
eternal life, must needs have the effect of convincing the

favored soul that sin will automatically cut him off from such fulfilment here and hereafter.

The speculative mysticism of Neo-Platonism found expression in terms acceptable to practical western Christianity in the writings of the pseudo-Dionysius, which were of course believed to date back to the age immediately following that of the apostles. Chief of these is the *Celestial and Ecclesiastical Hierarchy*, of which the first part treats of the way to God, leading from the lower creation up through the angels in all their ranks. These favored beings attain the end of all created things, the knowledge of God, by means of direct intuition; they perceive the divine essence according to the laws of their existence as pure intelligences. Dionysius explains that the second part of his work is called the *Ecclesiastical* rather than the *Earthly Hierarchy* because it, no less than the *Celestial*, has for its goal the knowledge of God, but of God as revealed in Christ incarnate. As man is by nature incapable of the direct intuition of God vouchsafed to the heavenly orders, he is entirely dependent on material symbols, by means of which he may attain such contemplation of God as his capacity allows. These material symbols are the sacraments intrusted to the hierarchy of the church, and so by sacerdotal functions he is led to the knowledge of God. Dionysius emphasizes three symbolic sacraments: baptism, representing purification; the eucharist, illumination; the holy chrism, perfection. Through the translation of Erigena (c. 800–c. 877), the theories of Dionysius had an important place in the religious thinking of the western church, and through them the entirely independent and individual ecstasy of the Neo-Platonist was brought within the bounds of ecclesiastical discipline.[1]

In the eleventh century, which saw Hildebrand developing the claim of the church to rule in matters temporal; and

[1] For citations from Dionysius, *vide.* App. p. 119.

adapting all the methods of statecraft and politics to the support of that claim, and which heard religious discourse reduced for the most part to the dialectic of the schools, Bernard of Clairvaux fanned into glowing life the undying embers of mystic contemplation and knowledge of God. His mysticism was of his age. As a schoolman he admitted certain externally imposed truths on which reason may act even if they may not be rationally understood, but within their limits man may, by the grace of God, know God and be united to Him. He too based "the ascent of the soul towards perfection on supernatural grace, the communication of which begins in the present life," [1] and he never doubted that this communication of grace comes through the church and its ordinances. Vindicator of orthodoxy against the great Abelard, he escaped the suspicion with which ecclesiastical authority is wont to regard those who claim direct — and undirected — vision, and so came nearer founding a school than any other of the great mystics.[2] The Victorines made use of all the logical apparatus of the day to systematize the mystic emotion of Bernard and so developed a complete code of the laws which govern the ascent of the soul to God. Bonaventura, continuing and developing that which the Victorines had laid down, carried to its highest pitch the union of great dogmatic theologian and fervent contemplative mystic. But even Aquinas, who stands as the embodiment of the scholastic system, reveals glowing mystic devotion in his hymns and prayers.

It would be expected that in this school of orthodox mysticism the special emphasis of the day on sacramental grace in general and particularly on that bestowed by the eucharist would have its effect, and, as a matter of fact, the names which are associated with the opposition to Beren-

---

[1] de Wulf, *op. cit.*, p. 215.

[2] For discussions of scholastic mysticism, *vide*. Inge, *Christian Mysticism*, p. 140, and de Wulf, *op. cit.*, pp. 212–218.

garius, and which are noted as authorities on eucharistic doctrine and worship, are those of the forerunners of the school, — Anselm of Canterbury, Hildebert of Lavardin, and, especially, Honorius of Autun. But it is to Hugh of St. Victor that we must look for the fullest and most important expression of the relation of sacramental grace to mystical experience, — a relation which, as we have seen, is found in germ in the work of Dionysius. The final blessedness of man is the *visio Dei*, but to this he may not attain without the grace of God received through the sacraments. Of these the eucharist is the supreme means of attaining the end, for in it figure and essence are one and the same, even Christ, Who is on the altar, though hidden beneath the veil, and Who is sacramentally received into the soul.[1]

It is very much easier to make a general statement of this devotion and its expression than to convey any real conception of its fervor and enthusiasm. But even a slight

[1] "Since mystics have, as a rule, the extreme susceptibility to suggestions and impressions which is characteristic of all artistic and creative types, it is not surprising to find that their ecstasies are often evoked, abruptly, by the exhibition of, or concentration upon, some loved and special symbol of the divine. Such symbols form the rallying points about which are gathered a whole group of ideas and intuitions. Their presence — sometimes the sudden thought of them — will be enough, in psychological language, to provoke a discharge of energy along some particular path. . . For the Christian mystics, the sacraments and mysteries of faith have always provided such a *point d' appui;* and these symbols often play a large part in the production of their ecstasies." — Underhill, *Mysticism,* p. 434, 5.

"God enkindles in the souls of contemplatives the light of contemplation which represents the manner and design by which the body of Christ exists under the sacramental species, as a king on his throne with a curtain or veil intervening, as a glorious sun shaded by the passing clouds, as a fountain of Paradise hidden by the leaves of the sacramental species, from which issue forth four rivers of grace, of mercy, of charity and piety, to irrigate, delight, and fructify the church and the hearts of the faithful who drink of the waters." — Godinez, cit. A. Devine, *A Manual of Mystical Theology,* p. 72.

acquaintance with the thought of these men is worth acquiring, for it helps in placing our minds, as far as may be, in a line with theirs.

Hildebert of Lavardin found in the eucharist the food of the pilgrim on his way to the fatherland, the banquet of man with angels, perpetual strength, and the union of the creature with the Creator. Through it is the soul worthy to be found among the sheep, chosen with the good fish, gathered into the garner of the Lord.[1] At the supreme point of his great work, *De Sacramentis,* Hugh of St. Victor thus summarizes the position of the eucharist:

"The sacrament of the body and blood of Christ is that in which salvation is chiefly to be found, and it is singular among them all because from it is all sanctification. For this is the victim perpetually offered for the world's salvation; this gives efficacy to all sacraments before and after it."[2]

The same mystic in one of his sermons [3] declares the eucharist to be the mystery which mitigates the inner sorrow of the living, heals wounds, drives out the enemy, delivers from evil, strengthens righteousness. It lessens the guilt of the dead, remits their punishment, opens heaven, and assures eternal life.

The whole emotional nature of Aquinas, "venerabilis sacramenti laudator Thomas summus," was poured out in eucharistic devotion. Not only was he the composer of the office for Corpus Christi day, with its series of unsurpassed eucharistic hymns, but his prayer before communion glows with mystical fervor.

"O most merciful Lord, grant that I may so receive the body of Thy only begotten son, our Lord Jesus Christ, which He took of the Virgin Mary, that I may be worthy to be incorporated into His

[1] *Sermo, Migne,* CLXXI: 604.
[2] II: viii. *Migne,* CLXXVI: 461.
[3] *Sermo* XCIV, *Sermones Centum, Migne,* CLXXVII: 1195.

mystical body and reckoned among its members. O most loving Father, grant me that Him Whom I, on my pilgrimage, now purpose receiving beneath a veil, I may behold with unveiled face throughout eternity."[1]

The same note of the eucharist as a pledge of ultimate bliss is struck in the prayer after communion:

"I pray thee that this holy communion may not be to me an occasion of guilt but may plead for my salvation: that it may be my armor of faith and shield of good will . . . my firm defence against the evil of all enemies, visible and invisible . . . my unshakable cleaving to Thee, the true and only God, and at the last my happy consummation. And I pray Thee, that Thou wilt hold me worthy to attain to that ineffable festival where Thou with Thy Son and the Holy Spirit, art the true light of the saints, full satisfaction, joy fulfilled, and everlasting felicity.[2]

The eucharistic prayer of Bonaventura is even more impassioned. To him the eucharist is bread of angels, refreshment of holy souls, our daily bread as well as bread of heaven, having all savor. By means of it the soul shares in the source of life, of wisdom and knowledge, the fountain of eternal life, the torrent of joy, the riches of the house of God.[3] The eucharistic prayer incorporated in the *Ancren Riwle* expresses the same idea, adopting the very words of St. Paul as to the enigmatic earthly vision which is the pledge of that which shall be face to face:

"Grant, we beseech Thee, Almighty God, that Him Whom we see darkly and under a different form, and on Whom we feed sacramentally on earth, we may see face to face, and may be thought worthy to enjoy Him truly and really as He is in heaven."[4]

---

[1] *Breviarium Romanum.*   [2] *Ib.*   [3] *Ib.*
[4] Tr. Morton. "Concede, quesumus, omnipotens Deus, ut quem enigmatice et sub aliena specie cernimus, quo sacramentaliter cibamur in terris, facie ad faciem eum videamus, eo sicuti est veraciter et realiter frui mereamur in coelis."

Eucharistic rapture is met with very frequently in records of mystic experience at this period. The Blessed John of Ruysbroeck, swooning at mass, explained, "Even today Jesus Christ appeared to me, filling my soul with deliciousness all divine; He said to my heart 'Thou art Mine and I am thine.'" [1] Catherine of Siena claimed knowledge of the Trinity in eucharistic transport,[2] and the Blessed Angela of Foligno, speaking of her mystic states, said, "One of the works which God Himself wrought in my soul is a power of comprehending, with great capacity and delight, how it is that God comes into the sacrament of the altar with that great and noble union." [3] Hildebert of Lavardin preached that the mystery of the conversion of the bread and wine, and of the grace conferred by it, could be contemplated by intuition, could be heard without sound of voice.[4]

While the inexplicable and unspeakable vision of God belongs to the higher type of mystic contemplatives, those on a lower plane always require a sign, and such signs are common in the religious experience of some mystics.[5] The crucified Christ of St. Gregory [6] is one of these, as is also the vision of a child or a lamb on the altar. Veronica of Binasco saw a marvellous light hovering over the chalice, Catherine of Siena saw Christ at different ages on the altar, Marie of Oignys saw at times a lamb, at others a dove, and visions like that of St. Gregory were vouchsafed to many people at Douay.[7]

---

[1] Dom Vincent Scully, C. R. L., *A Medieval Mystic*, pp. 40, 41.

[2] *Dialogue*, Ch. CXI, tr. Thorold.

[3] Cf. Algar Thorold, *Catholic Mysticism*, p. 159.

[4] "Solus hæc intuitu quodam contemplatur: audit sine strepitu vocis: de longe odorans, leniter tangens, avide gustans." *Sermo, Migne*, CLXXI: 604.

[5] *Infra*, p. 82.

[6] *Infra*, p. 78.

[7] Cf. Görres, *Die Christliche Mystik*, II: 107. Also Cæsarius of Heisterbach, *Dialogus Miraculorum*, Bk. IX.

Thus the mystics of the thirteenth and fourteenth centuries found the foretaste of the vision of God, the union with Him, within the bounds of holy church, consummated in the eucharist, in which banquet they knew both the joys of redemption and those of the heavenly country.[1]

IV

There remains the question as to how this matter of the development of a religious dogma with its bearing on worship and conduct concerns the student of literature. Why go into a mass of controversy which interests very few people today, and into devotional expression the undying part of which is incorporated into the general body of religious literature? So much of it seems to the modern reader exotic and exaggerated in feeling. But, surely, any literature worth studying must have been closely related to the life of the age which made it: nothing human is alien to it. As well conceive the literary production of the early nineteenth century uninfluenced by the theories of the rights of man as to consider the literature of the later Middle Ages apart from the sacramental system which received each man in infancy, which had a place for all the events of his life, and without which no man in Christendom willingly faced death. The climax of the system, the elevation of the host, was the heart of his Sunday and festival worship, and its hold on the popular mind is shown by the prayers and hymns for the elevation in various vernaculars.[2]

[1] Cf. a sermon ascribed to Hugh of St. Victor (*Migne*, CLXXVII: 956 ff). *In festivitate Paschali et corporis Christi*, in which the Passover supper is allegorized in detail. The eating of the passover in haste is thus considered with a play on words: "Comedamus festinanter ut mandata Dei, mysteria redemptionis, gaudia patriæ cœlestis cum festinatione cognoscamus. . . . Festinanter ergo comedamus, id est ad solemnitatem patriæ cœlestis anhelemus."

[2] *Vide* Mone, *Hymni Latini Medii Ævi*, I: 286, 293.

For the very reason that eucharistic doctrine and worship were so pervasive and enveloping, the literary records of them are seldom dogmatic explanations. It is not to poets and story-tellers that one looks for detailed theology, though one may safely assume for them a working knowledge of the church's teaching and an implicit faith in it. Just as in the illuminated missal the recurrent and familiar parts are indicated by two or three words, quite sufficient for the priest who knew it all by heart, so a very slight hint, the mere mention of a custom associated with eucharistic worship, a phrase indissolubly associated with the mass, a bit of the liturgy which could have but one meaning, an allusion to a popular belief or superstition — any one of these would suffice to show an audience of the twelfth and thirteenth centuries in which direction edification was to be sought.

One of the many examples of this is the passage in the *Perlesvaus* describing the taking of the Grail Castle.

"The virtue of Our Lord, and the dignity of the banner, and the goodness of the white mule and the holiness of the good hermits that made their orisons to Our Lord so struck the knights that they lost all power over themselves."[1]

This sounds like hopeless confusion and conveys no idea at all, unless we know that in popular speech, whatever subtleties the theologians might premise, the consecrated host is literally and locally Christ, that it was often carried in processions of intercession, and that a white mule was the animal preferred for such ceremonies.[2] Then our eyes too may see the picture which the romancer meant to call up to his audience, — the soberly clad group of hermits, probably singing their "orisons to Our Lord" as they moved slowly forward, the banner in the hands of Joseus the hermit, which indicated the coming of a King, a "vexillum regis,"

[1] Tr. Sebastian Evans, *High History of the Holy Grail*, XVIII: xxxii.
[2] *Cf.* Catalani, *Pont. Rom.* II: 313.

Perceval, knight of the Grail, bearer it would seem of the host, which at that date would be contained in a ciborium, or covered cup,[1] centre of the whole proceeding, the meaning and power of it so well known that even the foul knights of the King of the Castle Mortal quailed before it. No treatise on transubstantiation could show more clearly the place and force of the doctrine in medieval life. Explicit mention of the theology concerned is not needed: we do not ask that writers after 1859 mention the *Origin of Species* before we admit that they are more or less influenced by the theory of evolution. The burden of proof would rest on those who denied such influence.

The two following chapters are the result of an attempt to trace the bearing and influence of this most important feature of the daily life of the later Middle Ages, secular as well as spiritual, in two literary monuments. Both are concerned with religion, but, without any undue desire for classification, they may be taken to represent respectively the faith and devotion of the people and of the theologians — the *Legend of the Holy Grail* and the *Divine Comedy*.

[1] *Vide infra*, p. 59.

THE MYSTIC VISION IN THE LEGEND OF THE GRAIL

Li preudons "commencha la messe. Et quant il ot faite sa beneichon si prest corpus domini et fait signe a bohort quil viegne auant. Et il si fait sagenoille deuant lui. Et quant il i est venus li preudons li dist — bohort vois tu ce que ie tieng. Sire fait il oi bien. Je voi que vous tenes mon salueor et ma redemption en samblance de pain. . . . Mais mi oeil sont si terrien quil ne peuent veoir les espirituels choses . . . lors commencha a plorer trop durement." — *Queste del St. Graal.*

THE MYSTIC VISION IN THE LEGEND
OF THE GRAIL

I

The Grail quest is with us yet, as alluring and as illusory as at first, and the modern fellowship of the Grail, though composed not of knights but of scholars, is a large one. Perhaps the very fact that the questers are so numerous attracts new devotees. A problem which has so long interested so many must be worth solving, and as one after another the outer knots of the tangled skein are unravelled the chance of finding the master clew improves. It is not surprising that such a possibility brings newcomers to the task.

It would probably be admitted by all workers in the field that any theory of the Grail story, its origin and meaning, will have to reckon with numerous features which not only do not fit in with the theory but are in real or apparent contradiction to it. But it may also be admitted that the professional entertainers, empty singers of an idle day, who gave to the story the literary form which we know, were neither theologians nor literary historians. Their verse was perhaps at the disposal of monastic patrons and so adapted to a special propaganda, but their minds were stocked with the common properties of story-telling, and their task was to incorporate a certain amount of edification with a narrative sufficiently varied to command attention from an audience which asked only the beguiling of long hours. It is not hard to understand that any familiar phrase would bring up a host of images, the "sources" of which are probably much better known to the modern scholar than to the

medieval poet. Knights-errant might not arrive at their
goal without toil and test; so into the story of their adventures the narrator put any telling point, any emotional
interest, any decorative touch which the stored memory
happened to bring up.[1] In short, details of the Grail story
may have pedigrees of their own, respectable, even interesting, which are however merely hung on the family tree,
not really organically part of it. Because, for instance, some
elements can be shown to have close affinities with eastern
legend the origin of the whole matter need not be sought in
crusading influences. Or because a substructure of fertility
rites may be discerned beneath the Christian ritual we are
not thereby justified in inferring that the element of primitive worship is conscious or vital.

Though this study is chiefly concerned with the influence
of Christian doctrine and ritual on the Grail legend, it is no
brief for a Christian origin of the quest story. It would be
a difficult matter to shake the strong case made out by the
supporters of a Celtic origin of the story of a quest and a
fated question, associated with a magic vessel producing
food and a lance dripping blood. But this story was undoubtedly combined with another of an entirely different
origin, — that of Joseph of Arimathea, his care for Christ's
body, his guardianship of the holy vessel containing Christ's
blood, and his mission to Britain. The motive for the combination of two such elements, as far from each other in
character as in origin, has never been adequately explained.
It is this problem of the fusion of two stories that will be

---

[1] This is naïvely admitted in *Perlesvaus* (XX: xii), where we are
told that the very character of the country changed from time to
time so that knights might not weary of their quest. "Car, quant il
avoient entré en une forest ou en une ille où il avoient trouvé aucune
aventure, se il i venoient autre foiz, se trouvoient il recez et chastiax et
aventure, d'autre manière, que la poigne et li travaus ne lor ennuiast."
One suspects that variety was as important to the audience as to the
knights.

discussed in the present study, and the thesis to be maintained is that Robert de Borron, or a writer in Latin prose whose work was adapted to romantic purposes by de Borron, desiring to set forth the doctrine of transubstantiation and to establish certain local claims, combined the Celtic story of the quest with that of Joseph of Arimathea, derived from Christian legend. It required but a slight addition to the latter to identify the vessel in which Joseph received the sacred blood with the one used by Christ at the Last Supper, and such an addition may well have been suggested by the food-producing power of the magic talisman.[1] The change from a magic to a holy vessel would thus be pivotal.

An attempt to survey the whole Grail literature, even in the most summary fashion, would leave both author and reader with as little time as inclination for further pursuit of the subject. But as the texts are voluminous, and have, moreover, received various names at the hands of successive editors, it is absolutely essential to clear argument that the field involved be defined and that, for the purpose of this essay, one title for each version be fixed. A descriptive list of the various versions of the Grail legend with the name (in italics) under which they will hereafter be mentioned seems unavoidable.

II

Nutt's twofold division of the Grail romances is generally accepted.

"In the first, the chief stress is laid upon the adventures connected with the quest for certain talismans, of which the Grail is

---

[1] This trait which Miss Weston considers a hopelessly pagan feature persisting into the highly Christianized forms of the story (*Quest of the H. G.*, p. 64) seems to me the very feature to attract those seeking a romantic story as a vehicle for eucharistic teaching. *Vide infra.* p. 121.

only one, and upon the personality of the hero who achieves the quest; in the second, upon the nature and history of these talismans. The first may be styled the Quest, the second the Early History versions; but these designations must not be taken as implying that either class is solely concerned· with one aspect of the legend." [1]

QUEST VERSIONS

Conte del Graal. A vast poetic compilation in Old French. It was begun by Crestien de Troies and continued by other hands. The parts are usually designated by the names of their authors. Crestien's work c. 1180.

> **Crestien de Troies** (*Crestien*)
> **Wauchier de Denain** (*Wauchier*)
> **Pseudo-Wauchier** (*Ps-Wauch*)
> **Interpolation Ps-Wauchier** (*Inter. Ps-Wauch*)
> **Manessier** (*Manessier*)
> **Gerbert** (*Gerbert*)

Peredur, son of Evrawc (*Peredur*)

A Welsh romance preserved in a MS. of the thirteenth century. It was translated by Lady Charlotte Guest and included in her volume of the *Mabinogion*. Nutt estimates *Peredur* as in the main the oldest form of the Perceval story, but thinks that the form in which we have it is comparatively late (say 1230–1250), and that it has been influenced by the writings of Crestien.[2]

Syr Percyvelle (*Syr Percyvelle*)

An English metrical romance preserved in a MS. of the fifteenth century. No mention is made in it of the Grail nor of any other talisman. Gaston Paris believed that this poem represents the most authentic form of the original Celtic tale. Of its present form he said,

---

[1] *Legends of the H. G.*, p. 5.
[2] *Celtic Myth and Saga, Folk Lore*, Sept. 1892.

"*Le Syr Percyvelle* s'appuie certainement sur un poème *anglo-normand* perdu, et nous offre un spécimen des romans biographiques qui forment la plus ancienne couche des romans français du cycle breton." [1]

Parzival (*Parzival*)

Written by Wolfram von Eschenbach in Middle High German verse, (early thirteenth century). Wolfram claims as source a Provençal poet, Kiot.

Of these four Quest versions Nutt says:

"One French version (Crestien) speaks of the sword, a bleeding lance and a Grail (a vessel); another (if Wolfram's poem be regarded as representing a lost French original), of sword and lance and Grail (a stone); the Welsh tale mentions a bleeding lance and a head in a salver; the English romance is silent concerning any talisman." [2]

Diu Crône (*Diu Crône*)

In Middle High German verse, and written by Heinrich von dem Türlin. It is largely devoted to praise of Gawain, and includes fragments of very early traditions concerning him. In it the Grail is in one place a stone, in another a vessel containing the host.

EARLY HISTORY VERSIONS

Joseph d'Arimathie (*Metr. Jos.*)
(Called also **Metrical Joseph**
and **Petit St. Graal**).

Merlin (*Merlin*)

These two French metrical romances are generally ascribed to Robert de Borron. His work has been dated from 1170–1212: taking political and religious

---

[1] *Société historique et cercle Saint Simon*, Bulletin 2: 99, 1883. Cit. Miss Weston, *Sir Perceval*, I: xviii.

[2] *Legends of the H. G.*, p. 18.

conditions into consideration, I should be inclined to place it in the last decade of the twelfth century.

Joseph (*Prose Jos.*)

Merlin (*Prose Merlin*)

Prose versions of de Borron's poems with interpolations which Nutt believes were "designed to bring the text into conformity with later developments of the legend." [1]

Perceval (*Prose Perceval*)

This version appears in two forms, known as **Didot Perceval** and **Modena Perceval**. The first copy known is in a MS., which belonged to A. F. Didot, where it follows *Prose Jos.* and *Prose Merlin*. Another MS. in the Biblioteca Estense, Modena, is generally considered a superior text. Opinions differ as to whether this is a prose version of a lost poem by de Borron, intended to complete the trilogy, or whether it is merely an addition at the hand of one of the prose redactors of de Borron, carrying out a supposed intention of his. In any case it seems a logical and much needed conclusion to de Borron's work. For if the *Joseph* gives the early history of the Grail, the *Merlin* brings it into connection with Arthur's court. But this is only the prologue to the real romance. It is without meaning except as it provides the "great fool" of the Celtic story with a Christian object for his quest and makes the quest itself an adventure of the Round Table.

Grand St. Graal (*Gr. St. Graal*)

A very long French prose romance, so rambling and discursive that it never arrives at the accomplishment of the quest. It probably belongs late in the cycle.

Queste del St. Graal (*Queste*)

This French prose romance is the most theological and ascetic of the cycle. "It was embodied almost entire,

[1] *Op. cit.*, p. 25.

by Malory in the *Morte Darthur*." (Nutt.) [1] **As a matter** of fact, the omissions indicated by "almost" cover most of the spiritual and edifying matter of the *Queste*.

Perlesvaus or Pellesvaus (*Perlesvaus*)
(Called also **Perceval le Gallois**)

The time of greatest interest in the Grail, which is also the time during which the chief versions of the romance developed, may be set roughly as the last quarter of the twelfth century and the first of the thirteenth.

This French prose romance has been translated by Evans under the title of the *High History of the Holy Grail*. Evans, as also Potvin, its first editor, considers it the original version of the Grail romance, but many features, noticeably the change in the character of Perceval from lover and husband to celibate, seem to give the romance a very late place in the cycle. Its relation to the *Queste* is debatable. Is the celibacy of Perceval an imitation of that of Galahad? Or is the *Perlesvaus* "the transitional bridge between the knightly hero of Crestien-Guiot and the ascetic hero of the later legend," as Nutt believed? [2]

It is extremely important to note the marked difference between the two groups into which the texts fall — that which deals primarily with the Quest of the Grail and that which is most concerned with its Early History. Nutt felt that the diversity in tone and sentiment between the two is so marked "as to make the reader of the Early History versions feel as though transported into another world."

"The chivalric is here subordinated to the Christian ascetic element. True, the hero's prowess is insisted upon in set conventional terms, but the centre of interest is shifted from his personality and from the feats and ventures by

---

[1] *Op. cit.*, p. 30.
[2] *Op. cit.*, p. 75.

which it is manifested to the symbolic machinery of the precious vessel and its accompaniments. . . .

" These differences in tone and feeling, not to be appreciated save by those who read the original text, would alone suffice to negative the hypothesis that the two sets of romances are the dissevered halves of a homogeneous whole, or variant versions of a common original theme. The distinction between them is far more deeply seated."[1]

III

Critical opinion as to the origin of the story falls inevitably into two classes as sharply divided one from the other as the Quest from the Early History versions. In one are those who hold that the Celtic vessel of increase and the adventures connected with it were gradually and almost accidentally affected by Christian teaching introduced in successive redactions of the story by Christian narrators. In the other class are the exponents of a purely Christian origin of the vessel. They hold that it was from the beginning the vessel of the holy blood, and that its story, in some quite unexplained way, was contaminated by elements which are traceable to Celtic story-telling. Nutt's studies are the most important contributions to the first theory, while Birch-Hirschfeld is the most conspicuous defender of that of the Christian origin.

Quite recently a third theory has made its appearance, — the so-called "ritual theory."[2] This view "sees in the Grail tradition as preserved to us the confused and fragmentary record of a special form of nature-worship, which,

[1] Nutt, *op. cit.*, pp. 36, 37.
[2] It is confusing to narrow the word "ritual" to any special form of worship, primitive or otherwise. Golther's contention that the Grail worship is that of the Byzantine mass is also a "ritual" theory.

having been elevated to the dignity of a mystery, survived in the form of a tradition." This theory is earnestly upheld by Miss J. L. Weston, in whose words the statement above is given,[1] and has also a supporter in Dr. Nitze. Miss Weston, however, thinks the fertility rites connected with the worship of Adonis answer most closely to the details of the Grail story, while Dr. Nitze believes those associated with the Eleusinian Mysteries to be most closely affiliated.[2]

Details of the Grail story have been analyzed interminably. Innumerable studies of the dates of the various texts and their sequence exist. There are vehement controversies as to whether Bleheris and Kiot, mentioned in certain texts as sources, are to be regarded as real persons or literary fictions. Some critics are inclined to believe that Walter Map really had something to do with the later forms of the story, but Sommer in his edition of the *Grand St. Graal* and the *Queste* has stated his opinion that the ascriptions to Map are without foundation in fact. Many pages have been devoted to establishing the identity of Robert de Borron, without convincing results.

To such Celtic scholars as Alfred Nutt and A. C. L. Brown we owe careful study of features which can be paralleled in Celtic story. The elaborate work of Hagen is one of the latest efforts to determine the significance and value of the traces of the Earthly Paradise legend and other eastern material, and its possible connection with the Crusades. There are many valuable studies of the relation of the Grail ritual to the ritual of the Christian church, especially to that of the eastern branch. Among them may be mentioned those of Heinzel, Newell, Golther, and Miss Peebles. Wolfram's *Parzival*, with its marked differences from any other version, has called forth much scholarly

[1] *Quest of the H. G.*, p. 98.
[2] For discussion of this theory and of the relation of fertility rites to eucharistic worship, *vide.* App., p. 121.

work. The discussions of San Marte, Sterzenbach, and Hertz should be particularly noticed.

In all this outpouring of critical scholarship, the fusion of two distinct stories — that of the quest of a magic, food-producing vessel, and that of the vessel of Christ's blood, treasured by Joseph of Arimathea — is almost invariably regarded as the most important and significant point in the finished narrative, but there have been few attempts to find a credible motive for the combination. Paulin Paris considered that it resulted, directly or indirectly, from the desire of the Glastonbury monks to stand well with Henry II, but he viewed the Grail itself as nothing more than a specially holy relic and so a desirable possession.[1]

Potvin, who put the beginnings of the whole cycle much earlier than would any critic of the present day, saw in the *Perlesvaus* an "epic of theocracy," an Iliad of the genius of Hildebrand, whose claim to universal rule was thus upheld by the institutions of chivalry. He believed that Perceval typified civil war on behalf of theocratic government.[2] The supporters of the theory of an origin in fertility rites believe that a magic vessel was connected with these rites in pre-Christian Britain, and that a confused memory of this worship was carried over into the rites of the Christian church.

IV

To offer a theory with the avowed object of twisting many of these threads into a dependable clew to the maze is to display audacity far removed indeed from angelic hesitation. Such a theory must make use of all these lines of research. It may freely admit the Celtic origin and yet have a place for reminiscences of fertility rites and for the

[1] *Romania*, I: 482.
[2] *Introduction to the Conte del Graal.*

eastern elements. It must account for the varying form of the Grail, and have an answer for the question of the fusion of the two stories. Yet one ever-present idea, the desire to express one intense conviction, would serve to unite many loose ends, and like a scarlet thread might be followed through all the intricacies of the coil. And such a scarlet thread may well be the glorification of transubstantiation, for by the last quarter of the twelfth century that doctrine, after the long controversy just outlined,[1] had become a favorite subject for sermon and exposition, found expression in art, in ritual and in sacred poetry, and lent strength to the power of the keys.[2] It was emphasized in England by Lanfranc and his followers, and the Benedictines were particularly active in promulgating it. And during these twenty-five years we find the story of a miraculous vessel called the Grail becoming popular with the romance writers. Combined with the Christian legend of Joseph of Arimathea, which for some unknown reason was familiar in England at an early date, the story acquired in successive retellings an increasingly doctrinal and didactic character.

It may fairly be presumed that this steady growth of emphasis on Christian teaching reflects contemporary religious emphasis; and such a presumption leads to the suggestion that the Celtic story, with its symbols, was used as a foundation for the later Grail romances because it was particularly well suited to the double purpose for which it was intended — the glorification of the dogma of transubstantiation, of very special contemporary importance, and the establishment of the claim of England in general and

[1] *Vide ut sup.*, Ch. I.

[2] The withdrawal of the eucharist was one of the chief terrors of an interdict. Cf. Dante's accusation of the popes:

> They take away, now here, now there, the bread
> The pitying father would lock up from none.
> > *Paradiso*, XVIII: 128, 129, tr. Johnson.

Glastonbury in particular to early and independent connection with the dogma. On this hypothesis the Grail, at
least in de Borron's version of its story and in those modelled
on him, is the symbol of transubstantiation, the perpetual
miracle of the church by which man attains to the closest
approximation possible to one still on earth to that final
union with God which is the ultimate blessedness of man.
In accordance with this theory the *quest* of the Grail is the
aspiration for mystic intuition of the miracle, a direct
knowledge which, as we have seen,[1] is not faith, though
faith is an indispensable condition of its attainment. A
chosen few have achieved this sacramental mystic vision;
they "know how God comes into the sacrament."[2]   Others,
even among the faithful, must be content with faith, and
believe in the sacramental presence of Christ.

As a symbol of transubstantiation the Grail need not be
one definite object: its form may vary. For the romancer's
purpose any ritual accessory to the consecration of the
elements, — chalice, paten, ciborium, tabernacle, or altar
stone, — may represent the miracle of transubstantiation.
Each story teller may select that which appeals most to his
imagination, or which has special interest for him or for his
audience. For the actual material object is but a symbol, a
figure of the thing signified. The true Grail is indeed "chose
esperitel," "of wood was it not, nor of any kind of metal
nor of stone was it wrought, neither of horn nor of bone."[3]
This interpretation, it will be seen, offers an explanation
of the long discussed question as to why Wolfram described
the Grail as a stone, while in other versions it appears as
a dish or chalice.

This theory as to the significance of the Grail requires
support from without as well as from within. External

---

[1] *Ut sup.* p. 19.
[2] Angela of Foligno, *vide* Thorold, *Catholic Mysticism*, pp. 158, 159.
[3] *Prose Lancelot.*

evidence is to be sought in the emphasis on the doctrine of transubstantiation at the time of the development of the Grail romances, and the ambition of the Glastonbury monks to identify themselves as heirs of primitive British tradition, so that they might offer to Henry II in his struggle with the papacy such prestige as would accrue from direct knowledge of important doctrinal teaching and from a usage and ritual which claimed entire independence of the authority of Rome. Study of the texts themselves shows a constant association of the Grail with eucharistic ceremonial. It seems to be identified with one and another of the accessories of the mass, and there are striking resemblances between its effects and those of the eucharist. For example, the miracles which were related as evidences of transubstantiation appear in connection with the manifestations of the Grail. The great charge connected with the possession of the Grail is called its "secret," and the term suggested to contemporaries the words of consecration of the mass, words which effect transubstantiation, at that period called *secreta*. The later Grail romancers introduce the requirement of celibate chastity on the part of the Grail hero: this is done in *Perlesvaus* by transforming Perceval; in the *Queste* by the introduction of Galahad. The glorification of celibacy finds a parallel in the purity required of those who are connected with the ministry of the altar and the offering of the mass, a purity on which increasing stress was laid at the time those romances developed.

V

The conspicuous importance of the doctrine of transubstantiation at the time of the flowering of the Grail romances has been discussed in the previous chapter. When we take up the question of the connection of Glastonbury with the Early History versions, we are at once confronted with the problem of Robert de Borron and the trilogy of *Joseph of Arimathea, Merlin,* and *Perceval* generally attributed to him. Who was he? Hucher was sure he was "homme d'épée," in spite of his marked talent for theological exposition. Miss Weston claims him as an "initiate." Was he perhaps a jongleur turned monk, like Helinandus, or a jongleur officially attached to the monastery of Glastonbury, as Bédier would probably prefer to think him? Or was he a knightly singer, familiar with the ambitious claims of Glastonbury as well as with the weak points of the court? Whoever he was, it is hardly disputed that he is responsible for combining the Celtic quest story with the legend of Joseph of Arimathea, and for adding to the latter the identification of the vessel in which Joseph caught the blood of Christ with the dish of the Last Supper.

The *Metrical Joseph* begins with a theological exposition of the fall of man, death as the penalty of his sin, and the Incarnation as the remedy for it. The secret devotion of Joseph, who is represented as an officer of Pilate, is related. The narrative then proceeds to an account of the Last Supper. After it Judas leads the Jews into the house of Simon, where it had taken place, and there betrays his Master. In the confusion the disciples leave behind them the fair vessel with which Christ had instituted His sacrament. A Jew, however, picks it up and takes it to Pilate. When Joseph hears of the death of Christ he demands the body from Pilate. Pilate grants the boon and gives Joseph the vessel of the sacrament in which the blood from Christ's wounds is received. The story takes up the persecution of Joseph for alleged resuscitation of Christ, His imprisonment, the vision in prison of Christ bearing the holy vessel, from which a brightness streams. This He entrusts to Joseph after another long review of the fall of man and its remedy in the Incarnation. He also recalls the Last Supper, when the bread and wine were declared His body and blood, and promises Joseph that for his tender care of the sacred body the sacrament will never be celebrated without remembrance of him. It is explained that at these celebrations the altar [1] will represent the sepulchre; the vessel in which His body will be consecrated in the form of the host is to be called a chalice, and will represent that in which the sacred blood was received; the paten over the chalice is the symbol of the stone before the sepulchre; the cloth over both will represent the winding-sheet which Joseph used. Christ then teaches Joseph the great, "secret," which is called by the name of the Grail.

The next appearance of the Grail is in far distant lands, where it exhibits the power of separating the good from the bad, and we are told that the Grail is so called because it is agreeable to all who see it. There is much confusion as to the conversion of England and the guardianship of the Grail. De Borron's narrative at this point is ambiguous and obscure. At first long passages are devoted to Alain, descendant of Joseph's sister, and he is designated as the Grail-keeper. Yet he disappears from the story without explanation, and the chief rôle is assigned to Brons, husband of Joseph's sister. He is known as the Rich Fisher, is given charge of the Grail, and learns the holy words which the Lord spoke to Joseph in prison. In the metrical version no mention of Joseph as apostle to Britain occurs, though he

[1] W. W. Newell, *The Legend of the Holy Grail*, p. 25, calls attention to a passage in the *Gemma Animæ* of Honorius of Autun, first half of the twelfth century. "When are said the words *per omnia sæcula sæculorum* the deacon comes, raises the cup before him (the priest), puts on the cover, replaces it on the altar, and covers it with the corporal, representing Joseph of Arimathea, who deposited the body of Jesus Christ, covered his face with the sweat-cloth, laid it in the tomb, sealed with the stone. Here the oblate and chalice are covered with the corporal, which signifies the pure winding-sheet in which Joseph wrapped the body of Christ. The chalice designates the sepulchre· the plate, the stone which closed the sepulchre."

seems to send missionaries in that direction. But in the
prose (Cangé MS.) Joseph is said to have preached in the
land of Great Britain.[1] If the *Prose Perceval* is by de Borron [2] we find that in the *Metr. Jos.* de Borron has prepared
the way for the close association of the Christian vessel
with Merlin and the romantic adventure of the quest. The
Merlin is fragmentary, but it serves to bring in the court of
Arthur and the Round Table. In the *Didot-Perceval* Merlin,
almost at the outset, repeats the story of Joseph and his
guardianship of the Grail. The character of the Grail is
assumed as already well known, and the only feature specially mentioned is its power of separating the good from the
bad. Merlin says "Our Lord made the first table, Joseph
the second, and I, at the command of Uther Pendragon, the

---

[1] Joseph's mission to England is conspicuous in a Welsh version
of the *Queste*. Perceval's aunt relates how when Joseph of Arimathea
came to Great Britain, and his son Joseph with him, there came with
them about four thousand people, all of whom were fed by ten loaves,
placed on the table at the head of which was the Grail. In the *Gr.
St. Graal* Joseph brings his company to "angleterre" by means of his
miraculous shirt, and the Grail feeds the travellers.

[2] Nutt thought the *Didot-Perceval* an "incongruous jumble of
hints from de Borron's work and a confused version of the *Conte del
Graal*," intended to be a sequel to de Borron's poems. (*Legends of
the Holy Grail*, p. 34.) Sommer is also convinced that the author of the
Didot-Perceval is not de Borron, but an unknown compiler, and that the
quest of the Grail must have been carried into the prose versions from
some other source, i.e. a Perceval-Quest, other than the *Perlesvaus*,
but closely related to it, to *Crestien*, and to the *Queste*. (*Introduction
to the Vulgate Cycle*, p. xii.) If I understand Sommer, he assumes that
some one made a prose version of de Borron's two poems, *Joseph of
Arimathea* and *Merlin*, and added an adaptation of this lost Perceval-
Quest, carrying into it the Joseph-Grail-conversion of Britain machinery prepared by de Borron. But why may not de Borron have made
this concluding combination himself in a lost poem of which the contents survive only in the prose transcription? Certainly the two metrical stories which we possess escaped the same fate by the narrow
margin of one MS.

third." He also says the Grail is now in Britain, under guard of the Fisher-king, that he is sick, and will never be healed except by the intervention of a knight of the Round Table. Here is certainly a most ingenious combination. The holiest object in Christendom, the symbolic presentment of the chief glory of the church, the sacrament which was the focus of contemporary doctrinal discussion, is brought to Britain and connected with Arthur, the national figure in whom the reigning house was greatly interested. It needs for completion only the story of Perceval and his quest that the Grail may become the end and object of knightly achievement.

VI

A blend of Celtic folktale, Arthurian romance and the story of Joseph of Arimathea in the interest of theology and politics could originate nowhere in England so well as in Glastonbury, the oldest ecclesiastical foundation on the island. King Ine and St. Aldhelm laid the foundations of the Saxon monastery on a site which was already hallowed ground to their British predecessors. "Glastonbury became the channel through which there ran into the new and vigorous fields of English monasticism all the treasured legends and beliefs of earlier Celtic monasticism."[1] There, says Freeman:

"In the isle of Avalon, the isle of Glastonbury, the great Abbey still lived on, rich and favored by the conquerors as by the conquered, the one great institution which bore up untouched through the storm of the English Conquest, the one great tie which binds our race to the race which went before us, and which binds the church of the last thirteen hundred years to the earlier days of Christianity in Britain."[2]

[1] T. S. Holmes, *Wells and Glastonbury*, Ch. X.
[2] *Cathedral Church of Wells*, pp. 18, 19.

The monks may have enjoyed some favor from the conquerors, but in spite of it they had difficulty in maintaining their independence and prestige. In 1077 the last Saxon abbot was deposed by the Conqueror, and Thurstan, a Norman monk of Caen, was installed as abbot. He at once undertook to replace the local use in liturgy and chant by that of Fécamp, an ill-judged attempt which provoked riotous resistance, as may be imagined. Glastonbury later found a champion in Henry II, who was jealous of interference in English church affairs and grateful for any link with the past of Britian which might be helpful in his disputes with the papal see on questions of jurisdiction, — disputes which are too familiar to need more than mention.[1] In 1171, on his way to Ireland, he is said to have been a guest of the Abbey, where Irish harpers sang him the story of Arthur. In 1178 he took the ruling of the monastery into his own hands, and when the church with most of its ornaments and relics was burned in 1184, he undertook the task of rebuilding it.

The question of the alleged connection of Joseph of Arimathea with Glastonbury must now be considered. William of Malmesbury in his *Antiquities of Glastonbury*[2] recounts, with the usual vague mention of a more ancient chronicle, that St. Philip, bishop of Jerusalem, chose a band of new converts and despatched them, under conduct of Joseph of Arimathea, to the western world. They landed in Britain and converted part of the inhabitants. The king, Arviragus, ceded them a large tract of land where they built a church, Glastonbury Abbey. The implication is that once in England and at Glastonbury Joseph must have left his bones

---

[1] "Religion grew more and more identified with patriotism under the eyes of a king who whispered, and scribbled, and looked at picture books during mass." — J. R. Green, *Short History of the English People*, II: VIII.

[2] *Migne*, CLXXIX: 1683.

there. But from the time of Charlemagne the relics of Joseph of Arimathea had been the pride of the monks of Moienmoutier in the Vosges, until at an unguarded moment they were reft from them by "stranger monks," whom Paulin Paris shrewdly suspected to hail from Glastonbury.[1] Certainly in a charter inserted in the same book of the *Antiquities of Glastonbury* Henry II recognized the apostolic origin of the Abbey Church after an examination of the alleged title deeds which supported such a claim. So, without the slightest support from Gildas, said by Welsh tradition to have ended his days at Glastonbury, or from Bede, and without authorization from Rome, the monks of Glastonbury asserted that Joseph of Arimathea had come to England about the year 63 of the Christian era, that he had converted the inhabitants, founded Glastonbury, and, presumably, chosen that abbey for a burial place. Doubters could be referred to the venerable relics.

The monks, grateful for the king's belief in their long descent, requited his favor by an important discovery, nothing less than that the grave of Arthur was on their premises. According to the monk Alberic des Trois Fontaines the discovery was effected by an abbot who had the entire cemetery of the abbey excavated in the search, having been incited thereto by words which a monk had heard from the mouth of Henry II himself.[2] This certainly sounds suspiciously like a "command performance." But Henry died in 1189 and Alberic says this happened in 1193. If he is right the monks may have thought to interest Richard I in a discovery which would have made a strong appeal to his father. They certainly needed the new king's assist-

[1] Cf. *Romania*, I: 457 ff. In this article P. Paris cites the chronicle concerning the theft which left Moienmoutier desolate. *Vide.* App., p. 125.

[2] The citation from Alberic is given by San Marte, *Essay*, p. 17. For the full quotation, *vide.* App. 125.

ance in their fight against encroachment. Sometime during
the decade of this discovery, one Savaric proposed to annex
Glastonbury to Bath, and to be known as bishop of Bath
and Glastonbury. This plan would of course have deprived
Glastonbury of its unique position. The monks took their
grievance to Richard, who sided with them and encouraged
a fresh and successful appeal to the pope. They then
ousted Savaric and continued to enjoy their independence.

At all events, Glastonbury not only appropriated Joseph,
bones and all, as patron saint, but Arthur, grave and all,
as benefactor,[1] a combination which made both for the
glory of the abbey and for the claims of the church in
Britain to continuity and catholicity independent of
Rome.

It also tended to encourage the memory and practice of
every scrap of liturgy, ritual, or traditional custom which
belonged to the ancient church of Britain. Its ceremonial
differed markedly from that of Rome, but the exact nature
of its peculiarities is unknown, for the chroniclers content
themselves with the general statement that British customs

---

[1] It is interesting to note how gravely this assumption was accepted.
Giraldus Cambrensis (*Spec. Ec.* II: 8–10; *De Principis Instr.* I: xx.),
speaks of the ceremonies which marked the removal of Arthur's bones
to their new resting place within the Abbey Church. He further
observes that this discovery puts an end to the fabled disappearance
of Arthur into fairyland, a story for which he accounts on rationalistic
grounds. Glastonbury, he notes, was once known as the Isle of Avalon,
and it was to this island that Arthur's sister took him to be healed of
his wounds. Evidently, his wounds not healing, he died and was
buried there, as the discovery of his remains proves. By the next century the ceremonies at the removal of these remains had been trans-
ferred to the original interment, and we hear of the burial of the bold
king at Glastonbury by all the baronage of Britain

"With all wirchipe and welthe þat any wy scholde."
                                    — *Morte Arthure* (ed Banks), 4328 f.

were hostile to those of Rome.[1]   Aside from differences in
ecclesiastical usage there seem to have been customs of
doubtful morality.   Attention has been called by Miss
Peebles to the *agapetæ*, women who followed the Irish
missionaries and scandalized the Gallican bishops;[2] and in
Scotland barbarous usages connected with the mass existed
until they were indignantly abolished by St. Margaret.[3]
That these peculiarities, at least in the matter of ritual,
show sympathy with the Eastern churches seems to be indicated by scanty traces in art, architecture, and liturgy, as
well as by the claims of British bishops to consecration at
Jerusalem and by frequent references to the fathers of the
Eastern church, though it is very difficult to tell just how
much of this came through direct contact with the East
and how much through Gallican channels.[4]   At any rate

[1] "Britones toti mundo contrarii, moribus Romanis inimici, non
solum in missa sed in tonsura etiam." — *Gildas*, Ep. II. cit. Warren.
  "Qualis fuerit apud Britones et Hibernos sacrificandi ritus, non plane
compertum est.   Modum tamen illum a Romano divisum exstitisse intelligitur ex Bernardo in libro de vita Malachiæ cc. III, VIII. ubi
Malachias barbaras consuetudines Romanis mutasse, et canonicum
divinæ laudis officium in illas ecclesias invexisse memoratur."
                      — *Mabillon*, De Lit. Gall. I: ii: 14.

[2] *Legend of Longinus*, p. 209,f.

[3] "Præterea in aliquibus locis Scottorum quidam fuerunt, qui contra
totius Ecclesiæ consuetudinem, nescio quo ritu barbaro, missas celebrare
consueverant." — Theodoric, *Vita S. Margaretæ*, 8 f, cit. Warren.

[4] Cf. Warren, F. E., *The Liturgy and Ritual of the Celtic Church*,
p. 57 ff.   "There must have been originally some connection between
the Celtic and Oriental Churches.   But this connection need not have
been direct.   The most probable hypothesis is that Christianity reached
the British Isles through Gaul, and that whatever traces of Eastern influence may be found in the earliest Liturgy and Ritual of Great Britain
and Ireland are not due to the direct introduction of Christianity from
the East, but to the Eastern character and origin of that Church
through which Christianity first reached these shores.   There is strong
circumstantial evidence in favor of the immediately Gallican origin of
the British Church."   Among these evidences are adduced the adop-

these features, Eastern, primitive, or both, did not by any
means come to an end with the Norman conquest. Giraldus
Cambrensis was greatly concerned about them, though he
was, unfortunately, too good a pedagogue to dwell on
blunders.[1]

To Glastonbury there remained the task of presenting
to the world its splendid combination of saintly founder
and kingly benefactor, and its consequent claim to apostolic
origin and historical importance, and of making the story
acceptable to the reigning house. No better means of presentation than romance could have been found. Not only
were nobles and gentles accustomed to receive information
through the medium of romance, but there is strong prob-
ability that there were minstrels at Glastonbury, singers
and story-tellers, both monks and laymen, from the days of
St. Aldhelm, himself a singer, onward. According to San
Marte "King Edward prohibited monks from being rim-
ers or raconteurs, a sufficient proof that they frequently
appeared as such." [2] Warton has a good deal to say of the
connection between minstrels and monasteries. Sometimes
the monkish singers celebrated local heroes and Warton
says that the Welsh monasteries were the chief repositories
of the poetry of the British bards.[3] Jongleurs, not neces-

tion by the British Church of the Gallican psalter, of Gallican usage
in liturgy and ritual, the dedication of Celtic churches to Gallican
saints, the accounts which connect missions such as those of St. Ninian
of Scotland and St. Patrick to Ireland with St. Martin of Tours.

[1] "The maxims of the Roman canonists, introduced by the Normans
into England, had, as yet, found no favor among a poor, rude, and
illiterate clergy. It would have been of service to modern historians
had Giraldus thought it worth while to have entered into more specific
details of some of these peculiar usages. We might then have been
able to discover how much of old Celtic practice and belief still existed
side by side with a half-informed Christianity." — J. S. Brewer, *Int. to
Gemma Ecclesiastica*, p. xviii.

[2] *Op. cit.*, p. 30 n.

[3] I: 89–92.

sarily under vows, seem to have been attached to some monasteries. The charter of the confraternity of jongleurs at the Benedictine abbey of Fécamp still exists,[1] and the customs of Fécamp were very well known at Glastonbury.[2] Glastonbury singers had every opportunity for knowing the material of Celtic legend and custom. What more worthy of their skill than a narrative which should not only add to the prestige of Glastonbury but gratify royal patrons who were interested in showing that the church in England was not in any way indebted to Rome for her existence nor for knowledge of proper eucharistic doctrine and worship? Some such purpose seems to be indicated by de Borron, for the instruction given by Christ in prison is in full accordance with contemporary teaching,[3] and it should also be noted that emphasis is always placed on Joseph's original care of Christ's *body*. It is as a reward for that care that he is taught the "secret" words and is promised remembrance wherever the mass renews the sacrifice of the sacred body. No other saint than Joseph and no other relic than his sacred vessel could possibly have been so well adapted to the purpose of glorifying transubstantiation.[4] It makes

[1] Bédier, *Les légendes épiques*, IV: 15–18.

[2] *Vide. ut sup.*, p. 48.

[3] *Metr. Jos.* ll. 893 ff.

[4] That one element of the forces which made for the combination of all this material may have been a desire to rival the famous Saint Sang relic of Fécamp seems very likely, as there must have been at Glastonbury a more or less fat and ancient grudge borne towards Fécamp and its intrusions, a grudge which was probably not strong enough to interfere with judicious borrowings from its legend. This may be admitted without accepting in full Miss Weston's theory that "we have here in all respects, save the name, a complete Grail legend, and that going back to a very much earlier date than any of our extant Grail romances." (*Legend of Sir Perceval*, I: 161.) Fécamp claimed a miracle of a bleeding host, which is said in the legend to have occurred about the year 1000. But such miracles for the most part are of later date, and are part of the propaganda of transubstantiation. It is notice-

little difference whether this material was put together by de Borron, or whether he founded his romance on a Latin book emanating from Glastonbury.

The idea that story-telling was used to proclaim the glories of certain monasteries and that local scenes and characters were woven into the narrative is of course familiar as a theory of the origins of French epic poetry.[1] This theory places the birth of the *chansons de geste* in the eleventh century. To assert that in the next century a monastery utilized the later fashion of romance for the extension of its fame is to claim only a moderate amount of literary ingenuity for its scribes.

VII

The student of the Grail story finds no one of its difficulties more puzzling than that of the changing form of the Grail vessel itself, though it is noticeable that the romancers

able that the legend admits that the Saint Sang relic and the vessel of the bleeding host were concealed and not brought to light until 1171, when they were displayed in a blaze of illumination. It does not seem likely that this legend had other than local importance before the time of this great glorification, and the transubstantiation miracle certainly looks like a twelfth-century improvement designed to give special eucharistic significance to the relic of the holy blood. Glastonbury may have had a natural as well as an acquired desire to outdo Fécamp, but the motive behind both stories is very likely to have been to proclaim transubstantiation and to claim local precedence.

[1] Cf. J. Bédier, *Les légendes épiques*, IV: 475, 476. The author thus summarizes his purpose. "Rétablir la liaison entre le monde des clercs et l'autre, montrer que l'église fut le berceau des chansons de geste aussi bien que des mystères, revendiquier pour elles leur vieux nom délaissé, de roman de chevalerie, et marquer par là que leur histoire est inséparable de l'histoire des idées chevaleresques à l'époque capétienne, rappeler les faits psychologiques généraux qui provoquèrent en même temps qu'elles les croisades d'Espagne et les croisades de Terre sainte, en un mot les rattacher à la vie, c'est à quoi je me suis efforcé."

are apparently quite unconcerned about it. The word "grail,"[1] which Helinandus[2] translates *gradalis*, is said by him to mean a platter, wide and somewhat deep, on which costly meats are served. He also speaks of the Grail as the vessel of the Last Supper. Many write of the Grail as the dish whereon the paschal lamb lay. Crestien conceived it as a holy object, more or less vague, from which light streams. Out of it the Fisher king receives the host which sustains his life. The host is the consecrated wafer, and yet the Grail is said by many[3] to be the cup of the Last Supper, uséd by Joseph of Arimathea to hold the blood of the Redeemer, which must imply a vessel intended for liquid contents. At the very end of the *Queste* the host is taken from the Grail and administered to the company, which can hardly mean anything but that the Grail is here the ciborium in which the host was reserved for the communion of the people.

Wolfram von Eschenbach seems to attach a wholly different meaning to the Grail, for he calls it a noble stone adorned with jewels. In *Diu Crône* it is mentioned once as the tabernacle and once as a crystal monstrance. Always it has marvellous qualities, always it may come and go mysteriously, always it is associated with a miraculous supply of food and drink.

This study has already[4] proposed the theory that the Celtic vessel of increase and plenty, adapted to Christian purposes, became the symbol of the miracle of transubstantiation and that any accessory of the mass, intimately connected with the miracle, might be described as that symbol, in other words might be the Grail.[5] Chrestien was

[1] *Vide* W. A. Nitze, *Mod. Phil.*, XIII: 11.

[2] *Migne*, CCXII: 815.

[3] *Metr. Jos., Wauchier, Gr. St. Graal, Queste, Perlesvaus.*

[4] Vide, p. 42.

[5] In the *Queste* (ed. Sommer) the phrase "devant le saint vaissel" is in one MS. rendered "deuant lautel."

apparently unconcerned with dogmatic theology, or, perhaps, had the story-teller's instinct for the dénouement he never reached, but in his continuators, in de Borron, and in the versions dependent on his narrative, the connection of the Grail with the consecration of the eucharist seems clear enough. Let us examine some of the forms of the Grail in the light of this interpretation.

The identification of the Grail with the dish of the paschal lamb is taken by some critics as marking a distinct division in the romances. They consider that such an identification must exclude the conception of the Grail as the vessel of the Last Supper and of the holy blood. Helinandus says the grail is *cantinus* or *paropsis*, words which in the Vulgate are used indifferently [1] for the dish in which Judas dipped with Christ. The critics apparently assume that the dish of the sop indicates a vessel used for the Passover meal, with its roasted lamb, herbs, unleavened bread and wine, and not for the eucharist which followed it and which was instituted with bread and wine only. But *paropsis*, at least, certainly acquired a eucharistic meaning,[2] and it is not quite fair to expect absolute archæological accuracy from men in whose minds the type had been completely lost in the fulfilment.

Christ, "the Lamb that was slain," [3] is from the beginning absolutely identified with the paschal lamb, — Christ our Passover is sacrificed for us.[4] Thus logically Christ in the eucharist is the paschal lamb of the New Dispensation. This is reflected in ritual and in liturgies. In arranging for the preparation of the bread for the eucharist Algerus says that it is to be of the cleanest and purest, since it is to

---

[1] *Cantinus*, St. Matthew; *paropsis*, St. Mark.

[2] "Paropsis. Vas ecclesiæ ministeriis dicatum, idem quod *Patena*." Du Cange.

[3] *Rev.* v: 12.

[4] *1. Cor.* v: 7.

be transformed into the most glorious body of the immacu-
late Lamb.[1] In the Eastern liturgy of St. John Chrysostom
at the preparation of the elements for the mass the bread is
called "Holy Bread," or "Holy Lamb," and the deacon, after
laying the "Lamb" down in the paten, says to the priest,
"Sir, sacrifice."   The priest then, cutting it crosswise,
answers, "The Lamb of God is sacrificed, etc." [2] When the
host is offered in the Roman mass it is called "this immacu-
late victim" (hanc immaculatam hostiam), and the hymn
Agnus Dei was at one time ordered to be sung in connection
with the ceremonial fraction of the host. The host was
sometimes stamped with the figure of a lamb, lying down or
standing, and the vision of a lamb on the altar was one
of the eucharistic miracles.

The proper preface for Easter and the Easter sequence,
or festal chant between the Epistle and Gospel, contain the
same figure, as do also many pious treatises. In the Mitrale
of Sicardus of Cremona the paschal lamb is identified with
Christ and His presence in the eucharist.[3] This identification is found also in eucharistic hymns, Latin and vernacular,
and even in popular literature.[4] A letter of St. Catherine
of Siena to Messer Ristoro Cangiani [5] carries out the parallel
between the paschal lamb and the sacrament of the altar in
great detail: "Thus sweetly it befits us to receive this

---

[1] De sacram. corp. et sang. dom., II: ix., Migne, CLXXX: 827.

[2] Cf. Cath. Enc., Art. Agnus Dei.

[3] "Panis iste sacramentalis in carnem, et vinum in sanguinem tran-
sit: quia paschalis Agnus pro nobis occisus, carnem nostram a morte
redemit, et sanguinem fundens, pro nobis animam suam posuit, et
animam nostram quæ in sanguine habitat a criminibus expiavit."
Mitrale, III: vi, Migne, CCXIII: 117, 118.

[4] "ich meyne daz onschuldige lam,
    gotes froner lichnam."
    — Fronleichnam, Altdeutsche Schauspiele, ed. Mone.
    p. 163.

[5] Tr. Scudder, Letters of St. Catherine of Siena, p. 204.

Lamb, prepared in the fire of charity upon the wood of the cross."

But it may be objected that although to the men of the twelfth century the paschal lamb was more closely associated with the host on the altar than with the firstling of the flock slain for the Passover feast, there is still confusion as to which eucharistic vessel is to be identified with this dish of the paschal lamb. Is it the paten, or small flat dish covering the chalice, is it the chalice itself, is it the ciborium or monstrance? The answer is: any one of them, according to the immediate purpose of the writer or the local usage with which he was familiar. Innocent III, the pope of the Lateran Council, identifies the paten with the dish containing the slain victim,[1] and the figure of *Agnus Dei* is frequently used as a decoration for the centre of the paten.[2] In the eleventh century the host was broken on the paten, but in the twelfth century Durandus directs that it be broken over the chalice. This is explained by ritualists as intended to indicate that the blood in the chalice proceeds from the broken and mangled body of Christ. A portion of the host is then dropped into the chalice, to show that the body of Christ was not without blood, nor the blood apart from the body.[3] This sustains the point referred to below,[4] that both species contain the whole Christ. Therefore the chalice might also be considered the dish of the paschal lamb,[5] especially as the blood of the slain lamb figured prominently

[1] "Patena, quæ dicitur a *patendo*, cor latum et amplum signat; super hanc patenam, i.e. super latitudinem caritatis, sacrificium justitiæ debet offerri, ut holocaustum animæ pingue fiat." *Migne*, CCXVII: 834.

[2] Rohault de Fleury, *La Messe*, Pl. CCCXII, CCCXIII, CCCXVIII. *Vide* illustration opposite.

[3] Durandus, *De fractione hostie, Rationale divinorum officiorum*, IV.

[4] p. 62.

[5] Cf. Rohault de Fleury, *op. cit.*, IV: 119. Here the words "Ecce Agnus Dei" are on a chalice.

PATEN OF IMOLA - XI CENTURY ?

PATEN OF ST. DENIS - XII CENTURY

VARYING FORMS OF THE CHALICE.

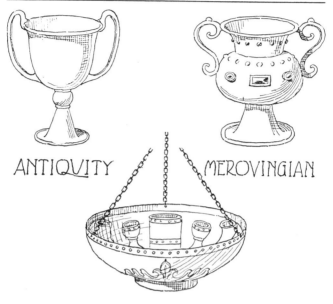

ANTIQUITY   MEROVINGIAN

BIBLE OF CHARLES THE BALD.

CHALICE OF ARDAGH ~ LIMERICK.
X-OR-XI CENTURY.

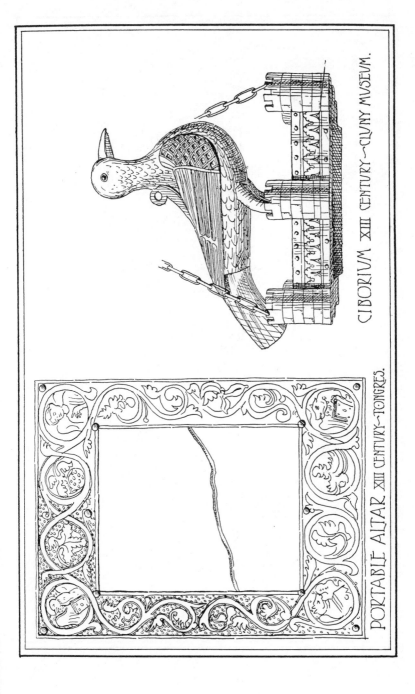

CIBORIUM XIII CENTURY~CLUNY MUSEUM.

PORTABLE ALTAR XIII CENTURY~TONGRES.

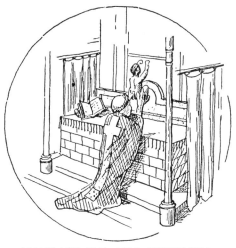

MINIATURE XV CENTURY
BIBLIOTHÈQUE NATIONALE.

CATACOMB of SS PETRVS et MARCELLINVS.

in the Passover ceremonies. Moreover "chalice" was loosely used for the ciborium or cup-shaped vessel in which the host was placed for reservation in the tabernacle and from which the people were communicated. The catalogue of the Stuart Exhibition (1889), listed a ciborium " known as the *'Cup* of Malcolm Canmore.'"[1] Giraldus Cambrensis, relating a miracle whereby the host was three times snatched from an impure priest, says the restored hosts were later found "in fundo *calicis*."[2] As late as the eighteenth century Martène speaks of the priest as carrying "*calicem* cum corpore Christi."[3]

The word "ciborium" has a curious history of its own, a history which can show transformations singularly like those of the word "grail" in the romances. Beginning as the Greek for the pod of the lotus, used, like the gourd, for a drinking cup, it came to mean the canopy over the altar. Later its original meaning of a cup became confused with the Latin *cibus*, food, and so ciborium comes to mean a dish (*vas*) for food.[4] Then it takes the meaning of the receptacle for the eucharist, either the cup with an arched cover, or the tabernacle in which this cup was placed.[5] Glass, mosaic, and illuminations show the host administered to the laity from vessels which are in no way different from chalices,[6] and there is, moreover, no uniformity whatever as to the shape of the chalice. Those made while they were still used to administer the wine to the laity are really loving-cups with two handles, and one of the tenth or eleventh century,

---

[1] *N. E. D.* (Ciborium), italics mine.

[2] *Spec. Ec.* IV: xxvii.

[3] *Ec. Rit.* IV: xxi: 8.

[4] "Ciborium vas ad ferendos cibos." — Ugutio of Pisa, cit. Du Cange.

[5] "Ciborium, pro Arca, ubi reponitur pyxis, in qua sacra eucharistia asservatur."— Du Cange. Cf. Rohault de Fleury, V: 89.

[6] Rohault de Fleury, *op. cit.*, Pl. CCLXIV, CCLXV. *Vide* illustration opposite.

from Ardagh, Limerick, is a two-handled bowl on a low foot much like the dish known to the trade as a "compote."[1]

Last of all these transferences is a local use of the word in Bavaria where it meant a portable altar, or altar stone.[2] This use inevitably brings up the form of the Grail as described by Wolfram von Eschenbach, the Bavarian.[3] A portable altar, *tabula altaris* or *altare portatile*, is a slab of natural stone large enough to accommodate all the vessels of the mass. Given a consecrated altar stone, mass might be celebrated in an unconsecrated building or out of doors. Such an arrangement was demanded in times of war and in unsettled parts of the country.[4] As might be expected, the number of portable altars increased notably during the crusades. The slabs were made of the more precious marbles, serpentine or porphyry, and in one example, at least, of rock crystal covering a picture of Christ on parchment. These were mounted in settings decorated with gold, precious stones, and plaques of goldsmith's work or enamel.[5] Ger-

[1] *Ib.* CCXCIX.

[2] Ciborium. "Parvum altare mobile, ut explicat Mabillonius in Itin. Germ. Quod Arnulfus imperator in castris gestari curabat, aureis laminis opertum, quadratæ figuræ, uno pede latum, altum duobus, præter turriculam, quæ in crucem desinit, quod etiamnum in thesauro Emmerammensis asservatur." Mirac. S. Emmer. tom. 6: 499. Du Cange.

[3] Theodor Sterzenbach, in his *Ursprung u. Entwicklung der Sage v. heiligen Gral*, 1908, declared his belief that Wolfram's grail was a "tragaltar." I reached my conclusion without knowing of his, and as my approach, evidence, and inference are quite different from his it is hardly necessary to say anything here of his views.

[4] "In itinere vero positis, si ecclesia defuerit, sub divo, seu in tentoriis, si tabula altaris consecrata, cæteraque ministeria sacra ad id officium pertinentia adsunt, Missarum solennia celebrari permittimus." Concilium Moguntiacense, ann. 888, cap. 9. *Mansi*, XVIII: 67.

[5] These altar stones are surprisingly small. That of Tongres, (*Vide*, illustration, p. 62), is said by de Fleury to be about 4×5 inches. Others are larger, but often not more than twelve inches long.

many inclined specially to these portable altars, and they were very numerous in Bavaria. The shrine of St. Emeran, apostle of Bavaria, at Ratisbon, possessed several, one set in a gold frame. After the time of St. Louis this type of altar stone ceased to be made. Abuses crept in and the permission to celebrate mass anywhere with such an altar was carefully restricted.[1]

Wolfram's poem is admittedly more closely related to the Crusades than any other of the Grail romances. To crusaders the portable altar, the altar stone with its splendid setting, meant the miracle of transubstantiation, the pilgrim's bread which was foreshadowed by the manna of the desert. It is not hard to understand its appeal to Wolfram as the most apt symbol for sacramental union with God, for the Grail.[2]

One or two further points of controversy as to the Grail itself, due to apparent contradictions in the legend, may be cleared up if the language of eucharistic liturgy and doctrine be considered and due allowance made for the passing of the ideas involved through the unecclesiastical medium of romance.

Heinzel thought that the sense of the Grail as a blood relic is lost in the sense of it as host, and that the paten, or flat vessel, is confused with the cup or chalice. In the *Queste* Galahad seems to receive *corpus domini* from the Grail itself. This difficulty is phrased by Miss Weston:

---

[1] *Vide* Rohault de Fleury, *op. cit.*, V: 1–47.

[2] Nutt says, "Be the reason what it may, Wolfram certainly never thought of associating the Grail with the Last Supper. But its religious character is, at times, as marked with him as with Robert de Borron or the author of the *Queste*." (*Studies on the Legend of the H. G.*, p. 251.) One may agree that Wolfram did not have the actual Last Supper in Jerusalem in mind, for he does not seem to have been concerned as to the early history of the Grail, but that is not to say that he had no eucharistic association with it.

"It cannot escape the notice of any careful student of the stories that between the version of Robert de Borron . . . and that of the *Queste*, a change has taken place: the point of interest has shifted from *contenu* to container; it is no longer the holy blood which is the object of adoration, but rather the Grail, the vessel in which the blood was preserved." [1]

If the Grail is the symbol of transubstantiation, it makes little difference which part of the sacrament is illustrated by it, for the whole Christ is present under the form of either bread or wine.[2] The numerous miracles of the bleeding host show the belief that the holy blood was contained in the host, and as a fragment of the host is always dropped into the chalice, it is easy to see how the symbol of the Grail may shift from chalice to paten, or even to monstrance and tabernacle, and still represent Christ under the sacramental veil. Moreover, though the host was consecrated on the paten or over the chalice, yet for the communion of the people it was, as we have seen, placed in the ciborium (a chalice-shaped vessel, but somewhat wider in the bowl), a

---

[1] *Legend of Sir Perceval*, I: 333. It strikes one as a little unreasonable of Miss Weston to refuse to the romancers the use of a metonymy freely employed by contemporary theologians. e.g. "*Hic calix.* Continens pro contento, calix pro sanguine, quia in calice sanguis. Calix in Scriptura pluribus modis accipitur. Aliquando per calicem sanguis Christi designatur, sicut hic, et in psalmo: 'Calix meus inebrians quam præclarus est.' (Psal. XXII.)" Baldwin of Canterbury, *Liber de sacramento altaris, Migne*, CCIV: 772.

[2] "Christus est verus Deus et verus homo, ideo consequenter est ibi Deus gloriosus in majestate sua. Hæc omnia quatuor simul, et singula tota simul, sub speciebus panis et vini perfecte continentur, non minus in calice, quam in hostia; nec minus in hostia, quam in calice; nec in uno defectus suppletur alterius, cum nullus sit; sed in ambobus in tegrum continentur propter mysterium." — St. Bonaventura, *Trac. de Prep. ad Missam*, I: 1.

In *Gr. St. Graal* Joseph takes from the paten "pièce en samblance de pain" and finds that it is "uns cors entiers." In *Metr. Jos.* Joseph told that the host is to be placed in a chalice.

practice which would account for Galahad's receiving the host from the Grail without any confusion between paten and chalice. Here the Grail is the ciborium, as it is also in any incident where it is seen on the altar, but not in connection with the actual celebration of mass, for the ciborium was used to contain the host reserved in the tabernacle.

VIII

Another point of discussion immediately connected with the Grail is that of the "secret" concerning it confided by Christ to Joseph in prison. About this de Borron is reticent, saying (in *Metr. Jos.*) he dares not go into detail about it as he has not the great book written by great clerks concerning it. In the prose version of the *Joseph* (Cangé MS.) the sacramental emphasis is stronger. The words are to be spoken only by one who has read the great book, and the secret is said to belong to the great sacrament made over the Grail, that is chalice.[1] The secrets appear also in the *Prose Perceval*. Alain is told by the voice of the Holy Spirit that he shall learn the secret words that Joseph knew. In the *Queste*, where the eucharist is administered by Christ, He assures the knights that He can no longer hold any part of His secrets from them.[2] He then feeds all from the Grail.

According to Durandus, the great expositor of ritual, the silent recital of the canon of the mass, the prayer of consecration, is called the *secreta*.[3] The reason commonly assigned

[1] "Ce est li secrez que l'en tient au grant sacrement que l'an feit sor lou Graal c'est-à-dire sor lou caalice."

[2] "Si conuient que vous vees partie de me reposatilles et de mes secres." ed. Sommer, p. 190.

[3] *Op. cit.*, IV. In modern Roman use, though the canon is still recited secretly, the word *secreta* is confined to the prayer said in a low voice by the celebrant at the end of the offertory. This restriction is really the earlier usage, the extension of the term to include the canon being medieval.

for this secret rendering is that the consecration is an exclusively priestly function.[1]

This contemporary meaning of "secret," which is certainly indicated in *Prose Jos.*, seems to make it fairly clear that the words whereby the miracle of the eucharist is to be performed are intrusted to Joseph, but it is not difficult to conceive that the word "secret" might come to be applied to the miracle itself.   As a matter of fact, in a contemporary treatise, the *Mitrale* of Sicardus of Cremona, who was flourishing at the time of the Lateran Council, it is so used.

"A mystery of faith, since one thing is seen and another is known, the species of bread and of wine is perceived, the body of Christ and His blood believed.   In Greek a mystery, in Latin a *secret*." [2]

A mystery, technically speaking, "is a supernatural truth, one that of its very nature lies above the finite intelligence." [3] The doctrines of the Trinity and of the Incarnation are two of the chief mysteries of faith, and transubstantiation is here declared by Sicardus to be another, thus according with the symbol of the Lateran Council.   So the "secret of the Grail" may very well be not only the words of consecration but also the miracle of transubstantiation performed by

[1] "Secreta ideo nominatur, quia secreto dicitur, et solius est sacerdotis soli Deo offerre sacrificium."— Hildebert of Lavardin, *Lib. de expositione missæ*, *Migne*, CLXXI: 1159.

[2] "*Mysterium fidei*, quoniam aliud videtur et aliud intelligitur, species panis et vini cernitur, corpus Christi et sanguis creditur. Mysterium Græce, Latine *secretum*."

— *Migne*, CCXIII: 130.

[3] Cf. *Cath. Enc.*, *Art. Mystery*. Also Mone, *Hymni Latini*, I: 270–273. Gawain's vision (*Perlesvaus*, VI: iii), and the hermit's interpretation of it (*Ib.*, VI: xii), seem an allegorical rendering of the mystery that after consecration the *substance* of bread and wine are replaced by the *substance* of the body and blood of Christ. This miracle is said to be the secret of the Savior, to be revealed only to those selected for such honor.

them. Certainly, when one considers the vast bulk of literature, didactic and devotional, on the subject it is not surprising that de Borron shrank from entering more explicitly into controversy about it.[1]

[1] On this matter of the "secret of the Grail" I take issue squarely with Miss Weston. (*Legend of Sir Perceval*, II: 232, 233.) She first speaks of the secret as confided by Joseph to Brons and by Brons to Perceval, ignoring the fact that it was first of all confided to Joseph by Christ in immediate connection with sacramental directions. (*Metr. Jos.*) So there is a eucharistic association with the secret from the beginning. She then draws attention to the "awkward fact that the formula of consecration is not, and never has been, secret." This dodges a still more awkward fact, for whether the words of consecration are or are not secret they are so called in medieval usage. Durandus, the great ritualist, so calls them, and there is no difficulty in finding numerous examples. The word is extended by Du Cange to the *tabella*, or tablet on which the canon of the mass alone was written and which was placed on the altar for the convenience of the priest. Miss Weston apparently confines the meaning of "secret" to that which is not known. But the word also bears the meaning of that which is not understood, the mysterious, in classical and Low Latin and in Old French as well as in modern French and English. Du Cange cites Hugh of St. Victor, "Sacramentum quomodo altera notione intelligi dixit quasi scilicet sacrum secretum, velut Sacramentum Incarnationis." *Sacramentum*, *mysterium*, *secretum* all convey the idea of that which is not comprehended by human reason.

Miss Weston's main contention is that if the Grail writers meant by "secret" the words of consecration they meant to discredit the authority of the church at large to receive and transmit the formula. But to recount the special eucharistic instruction and explanation given by Christ to Joseph is not to declare that this was the only orthodox explanation ever vouchsafed on the subject. St. Paul claimed for himself first-hand revelation as to the eucharist and its ceremonies, or, at least, such is the ordinary interpretation of *1. Cor.* xi: 23 ff., but he did not mean that this invalidated the teaching and practice of the apostles who were present at the Last Supper, nor did any one so understand him. The romancers claim only equal, not exclusive revelation for the church in Britain.

Elsewhere (*Ib.*, II: 300) Miss Weston opposes the identification of the mystery of the Grail with that of the eucharist, arguing that in such case Perceval would have achieved the quest when he made his

IX

A minor question in Grail criticism is that of the occasional glimpses of the legend of the Earthly Paradise which are found here and there in the Grail romances.[1] The country side restored to fertility by the achievement of the Grail is usually compared to the Earthly Paradise. In *Parzival* the hero partakes of its fruits on his first visit to the Grail castle, and in *Gerbert* the sword of the Grail castle is broken in the attempt to force an entrance to Paradise. One of Bohort's adventures in the *Queste* is concerned with the bird on the dead tree, which pierced its own breast that its young might be sustained with the blood, and the hermit explains: "There was the token and likeness of the Sangreal appeared afore you." [2] This instance of the dead tree and the birds is found in one of the Paradise stories, the journey of Seth to the Earthly Paradise.[3]

In *Perlesvaus*,[4] the Grail castle is called Edain and it is watered by the rivers of Paradise. Any souls dying therein are sure of the heavenly Paradise. This transformation of

communion on Easter day. I do not contend that the Grail is the eucharist, but that it is the symbol of transubstantiation which gives the eucharist its validity and which is accepted by the ordinary communicant by faith. Perceval, who has been excommunicate for seven years, must regain the privilege of sacramental communion by means of penitence and faith before he can hope to go on to the quest of mystic knowledge of the miracle.

I cannot, therefore, feel that Miss Weston has stated the position in plain terms nor refuted it. She is too obviously preparing the ground for her theory of de Borron as an initiate of a survival of fertility mysteries, and has ignored very important points both in her statement and in her refutation.

[1] Cf. *Sir Gawain at the Grail Castle*, ed. J. L. Weston, p. 81 n.

[2] *Morte Darthur*, XVI: xiii.

[3] Cf. Graf, Arturo, *Il mito del Paradiso terrestre*, in *Miti, leggende e superstitioni del medio evo*, I: 76 ff.

[4] XXII: i ff.

the garden into a city or castle is not by any means unique, and Graf connects it with the apocalyptic description of the heavenly city, the Paradise of God.[1] For though the literal Earthly Paradise was viewed as a spot having geographical location to the eastward, which might some day be found by a lucky traveler, it had also its symbolic meaning which was at least as important as the literal. The Earthly Paradise symbolized the church, with baptism its river, Christ its tree of life, the fruit thereof the eucharist.[2]

So the Grail castle may well be called Edain for a better reason than is suggested by Iselin, who considers the name only a poetic figure of speech indicating a condition of joy and peace.[3] It is allegorically the church, and when the Grail is restored to it, when the true value is placed on the eucharist and its spiritual gifts, then the barren wastes shall blossom as the garden of Eden.

Another indication that the Grail castle is a figure of the church is that its innermost gate is described as a rood screen, the usual division between the nave and the choir, beyond which is the altar. Gawain, looking at the gate, sees Our Lord stretched as it were upon the cross, with His Mother on one the side, and St. John on the other, and the figures were all of gold with rich stones which glowed like flames.[4] The figures on a chancel screen are almost invariably arranged in this way.

[1] *Op. cit.* I: 19.

[2] *Vide infra.* p. 92.

[3] *Der morgenländische Ursprung der Grallegende.*

[4] *Perlesvaus,* VI: xv. Gawain "esgarde la porte contremont et voit Nostre Seignor escrit si comme il fu mis an la croiz, et sa mère d'une part et seint Jehanz d'autre."

X

One of the most striking points in the development of the Grail romances is the change in the status of the hero of the quest. Perceval comes to us out of the Celtic past as lover and husband, but goes from us in the *Perlesvaus* consciously and aggressively chaste, with a chastity which is uncompromisingly identified with celibacy.[1] This condition is said to be absolutely essential; without it Perceval must fail as did Lancelot.[2] De Borron apparently had the same idea in *Metr. Jos.* when he made Alain deliberately choose not to marry. The celibate chastity of the hero is a fundamental part of the *Queste*, and one which the reader is never allowed to forget. Here it is embodied — if that is not too material a word — in the blameless and bloodless Galahad, who takes the centre of the stage, and thanks to Malory and Tennyson, has succeeded in keeping it as far as English readers are concerned. This matter is either casually put aside by scholars as a mere consequence of monkish ideas of chastity, or is carried very far afield. Rhys thinks it originated in the "shyness of Cuchulainn," and Miss Weston finds in it a parallel to a feature in the Hindoo cosmogony.[3]

---

[1] XXXII: xxi. (Perceval) "quar il ne perdi onques sa virginité pour fame, ce dist Josephus; ainz morut vierge et chastes et nez de son cors."

XI: iii. "Perceval, ce dit l'estoire, fu mout honoré el chastel la réine des Puceles, qui mout estoit de grant beauté. La réine l'amoit de mout très grant amor, mès ele savoit bien qu'ele n'an aroit jà son désirrier, ne dame ne damoisele qui s'antente i méist; car il estoit chaste et en chastéé vouloit morir."

[2] Cf. *Perlesvaus*, X: xv. "Li rois hermites li demande se il avoit véu le Graal, et il li dist que nanil. Je sais bien, fet il rois, por quoi ce fu. Le vos fuissiez en autre tel désirrier de véoir le saint Graal conme vos estes de véoir le réine, vos l'éussiez véu."

[3] *Legend of Sir Perceval*, II: 280. Her argument is that in spite of Alain's refusal to marry he appears, without any explanation, as father of the Grail winner, and that the same is true of Narada, son of Brahma.

Is it not, however, conceivable that both these analogies go back to a primitive custom which reached the Land of the Grail by the highroad of Jerusalem and Rome? A recent writer says:[1] "During the actual performance of sacred rites, chastity is almost everywhere exacted." It should be noted that in this there is something quite different from the hermit's seclusion; the sacrificing priest, and even the attendants at a sacrifice, bring their own gift of renunciation to join with the offering. This universal idea found its place in Jewish worship. Temporary chastity as a qualification even for laymen engaged in special religious exercises is indicated.[2] Moreover, though the Jewish priesthood was hereditary, the priest was ceremonially purified before his term of actual service and lived in cloistral seclusion in the sacred precincts while it lasted. Both ideas were familiar in the early days of Christianity. Says Mrs. Parsons: "In imitation of the Jews, ceremonial continence during his actual ministration was probably required of the priest from the beginning."[3] St. Jerome preached the superiority of the ascetic life in general, but exhorted the priests in particular, that as the Christian priest is always on duty, it therefore behooves him to be always chaste.[4]

The history of the struggle between ecclesiastical ideas and human nature is to be read in the proceedings of almost every council, but by the tenth century clerical morality was at a pretty low ebb.[5] Authorities differ as to the extent of marriage, more or less explicit, among the clergy, but certainly it was to be found in the regions remote from the

[1] "John Main," *pseud.* Elsie Clews Parsons, *Religious Chastity*, p. 215.

[2] Cf. *Exodus*, xix: 15; *1 Samuel*, xxi: 4.

[3] *Ib.*, p. 258.

[4] *Adversus Jovianum*, I: 34.

[5] Cf. Lea, *Historical Sketch of Sacerdotal Celibacy*, XIII, XIV: Herbert Thurston, *Cath. Enc.* Art. *Celibacy*. Ch. Oulmont, *Les débats du clerc et du chevalier*, pp. 24 ff.

centres. It was to Gregory VII (Hildebrand), that his immediate successors gave the honor of introducing, or of reënforcing, the absolute chastity of the ministers of the altar.[1] This determination of Gregory is generally attributed to his desire to solidify the power of the Holy See by assuring it a body of ministrants who had no interests apart from it. While there can be little doubt that the political motive was strong, it is worth noticing how often the service of the altar is connected with the pleas for celibacy. Innocent III scored those who would serve both Venus and Virgin.[2] After the same fashion Hildebert of Lavardin exhorted the clergy to maintain their purity as befitting those who were entrusted to pronounce the words which effect transubstantiation.[3] And this is generally agreed to be the first use of the term "transubstantiation," though not, of course, the first expression of the doctrine. This feeling is reflected also in popular satire.[4]

In spite of Gregory's determination to discipline the clergy in all parts of the world, reform lagged in outlying

[1] "Sed nec illi, qui in crimine fornicationis jacent, missas celebrare, aut secundum inferiores ordines ministrari altari debeant." — Council of Rome, 1074. *Mansi, Con. Col.*, XX: 404.

[2] "Quidam nocte filium Veneris agitant in cubili, mane filium Virginis offerunt in altari. Nocte Venerem amplexantur, mane Virginem venerantur." *Migne*, CCXVII: 368.

[3] *Sermon, Migne*, CLXXI: 772 ff. For text *vide* App.

[4]   Tu sacerdos huc responde
       cuius manus sunt immunde,
       qui frequenter et jocunde
       cum uxore, dormis unde
       surgens mane missam dicis
       Corpus Christi benedicis
       scire velim causam, quare
       sacrosanctum ad altare
       statim venis immolare
       virgis dignus vapulare.
               — *Carmina Burana*, ed. 1847, p. 36.
Cf. also poems by Walter Map, *Camden Society*, 49, 50.

parts of Britain, especially in Wales and the Marches thereof. "Romish discipline and ecclesiastical system had never fully prevailed in Wales. . . . Marriage prevailed generally among the clergy, allowed, but not named. Every clergyman appears to have followed the custom of having a female attendant to take care of his house, whom Giraldus, in the language of the canonists, calls a *focaria;* to all intents and purposes a wife. Of course no marriage rites could be celebrated between the parties in the face of the church." [1] Giraldus himself gives a vivid glimpse of the canons of St. David's and their excessively domestic preoccupations.[2]

In the *Gemma Ecclesiastica* [3] Giraldus devotes the greater part of Distinction II to clerical chastity, which he perfectly well knew to be a thorny question. Indeed he is somewhat inclined to consider the prohibition of clerical marriage a device of the devil. Nevertheless, in the unsavory state of things he can do no less than exhort the clergy to a rigid keeping of the ecclesiastical law, and the heart of his exhortation is the unfitness of the impure priest to consecrate the eucharist. In the *Speculum Ecclesiæ,*[4] Giraldus is quite as emphatic. Starting with the Jewish requirement of ceremonial chastity, he asks if as much is not required of those who consecrate at the altar, not the flesh of bulls and of kids, but the Lord Himself and true lamb, not in shadow and figure, but in truth.[5]

The requirement of chastity was extended from the sacrificing priest to those in minor orders and others who assisted him. Giraldus relates a story of sacrilege rebuked by a miracle where the offender is an acolyte who during

---

[1] Brewer, J. S., *Giraldi Cambrensis Opera*, II: xli, xlii.

[2] *De jure statu Menevensis Ecclesiæ*, Dist. I. *Ib.* III.

[3] *Ib.* II.

[4] Dist. IV: xxiii. *Ib.* II.

[5] "Sed Dominum ipsum agnumque Paschalem verum, non umbratilem illum et figuralem, sed realem."

mass let his glance stray to a woman.[1] Cæsarius of Heisterbach tells of the detection of a nun who continued to wash the altar linen after she had broken her vow of chastity.[2] So the celibacy required of the Grail keeper and of the knight who would achieve the quest is seen to have close affinities with the ceremonial purity of the officiant at a sacrifice, a requirement which was the subject of much contemporary exhortation. Local conditions may have sharpened the point, for the Glastonbury monks, whose monastic vows of course included chastity, were in perpetual and scornful disaccord with their neighbors, the secular canons of Wells, whose cherished privilege of separate dwellings favored the presence of *focaria* as described above;[3] a condition of affairs tending to arouse suspicion and recrimination.

In the prose romances there is no doubt whatever as to the motive of the chastity. In *Gr. St. Graal* Joseph is told by the voice of Christ that he is to have charge of the flesh and blood of the Saviour, because he is proved and known to be more free from natural sin than any mortal flesh can conceive.[4] In the same romance Joseph delegates his office to Alain, twelfth son of Brons, because of his virginity.[5] The coming of Galahad is also foreshadowed — the ninth descendant of Nascien will be perfectly chaste, will possess all virtue and behold the wonders of the Grail.[6]

---

[1] *Gemma*, II: xvi.   [2] *Dialogus miraculorum*, IX: lxvi.   [3] p. 71.

[4] "Car iou tai proue et conneu por le plus net de tous natureus pecies que nule morteus char ne poroit penser." ed. Sommer. p. 31.

[5] "Je vous otroi boinement a estre ministres del saint graal et encore pour ce que vous aues uoe si haute et si fort (e) chose a uostre oes comme uirginite vous otri ie que vous aies la signourie del sant uaisel que vuos maues demande si que vous en soies sires apres ma mort." ed. Sommer, p. 249.

[6] "Il sera uierges tous les jours de sa uie et en la fin de lui si sera si meruielleuse que de cheualier mortel qui a son tamps soit ni aura nul qui a lui soit samblables." ed. Sommer, p. 207.

Here we have chastity as a requirement not only for the keeper of the Grail but also for those who would achieve a sight of it. This appears in *Perlesvaus* when Perceval laments the failure of Gawain and Lancelot and the hermit answers: "Fair nephew, had they been chaste as are you, well might they have entered on account of their good knighthood." [1] Lancelot's unworthiness is sternly dealt with by late romancers. In the *Perlesvaus* he learns that unrepented sin in his heart, his love for the queen, will always come between him and the Grail.[2] In the *Queste* he is told that even if the Grail were before him, he would as little see it as a blind man would a sword,[3] because in spite of his many virtues he has lost chastity.

As has been said, the chastity of Galahad becomes almost the *motif* of the *Queste*, and through Malory's use of it the central point of Tennyson's conception of the Grail story. From a ceremonial requirement, symbolical of the purity of heart required of those who would see God, it gradually becomes a condition of knightly prowess, the reason why a tough lance thrusteth sure. But the medieval romance never so confuses the physical and the spiritual. Lancelot's sword arm is not weakened by his sin. But at Galahad's supreme moment we are again told that it is because of his virginity that he is permitted to know the marvels of

[1] XVIII: xviii.

[2] X: x. "Mès itant vos veil-je bien dire, se vos gisiez en l'ostel li roi Peschéor, que du Graal ne verroiz-vos mie por le mortel péché qui vos gist el cuer."

X: xii. "Mès li contes tesmoigne que li Graaus ne s'aparut mie à celui mangier. Il ne demora mie por ce que Lanceloz ne fust un des III chevaliers del monde de plus grant renon et de greignor force; mès por le grant péché de la réine qu'il enmoit sanz repantir, quar il ne panssoit tant à nule riens conme à lui, ne n'an povoit son cuer oster."

[3] "Se li saint graaus venoit deuant vous ie ne quit pas que vos le peussies veoir noiant plus que vns auugles feroit vne espee qui deuant ses iex seroit." ed. Sommer, p. 88.

the Grail. Not physical prowess but spiritual enlightenment is dependent on purity.

In view of this ceremonial tradition and theory, persistent and true to type in spite of the encroachments of human
frailty, it seems hardly necessary to wait for a possible Celtic
precedent with Nutt,[1] or with Miss Weston to suppose de
Borron to be an "initiate" of anything more remote than
ecclesiastical rule and ideal. In the early days of British
Christianity there must have been many instances of the
sons of the clergy taking their father's office, even though a
ceremonial continence had been exacted. A later writer
puts in rigid virginity, the requirement of his day, and
neither knows nor cares for the resulting discrepancy. It
may be observed, in connection with Miss Weston's theory
of Eastern influence, that Eastern asceticism generally sup-
poses a preceding married state.[2]

XI

There are so many miracles of one kind or another in
medieval romance that one ceases to pay much attention to
their details. It should, however, be noted how close is the
correspondence between the miracles ascribed to the Grail
and those which were brought to the support of transubstantiation. St. Augustine defined a sacrament or mystery
as that in which one thing is seen, another known (*aliud
videtur, aliud intelligitur*), and it would be hard to better
the definition. But when controversy is raging, human

---

[1] "No Celtic tale I have examined with a view to throwing light
upon the Grail romances insists upon this idea, but some version,
now lost, may possibly have done so. Celtic tradition gave the
romance writers of the Middle Ages material and form for the picture of human love; it may also have given them a hint for the opposing
idea of chastity."— *Studies on the Legend of the H. G.*, p. 247.

[2] Cf. *Hastings Enc.*, Art. *Celibacy*.

nature loses patience and asks for a sign. There is always a desire to finish up the opposition. Therefore we find that after the Berengarian controversy accounts of eucharistic miracles multiplied.[1]

These miracles fall into distinct groups. The most common is that of bleeding host, or the manifestation of real flesh on the altar. A doubter, priest or layman, a sacrilegious Jew, a devout man craving a special favor of God, finds the host bleeding. Fécamp has such a story, Brussels celebrated the Feast of the Bleeding Host (in this case a Jewish sacrilege is involved), and the miracle of Bolsena is unforgotten because of Raphael's treatment of it in the Vatican *stanze*. Other cases are recounted by Cæsarius of Heisterbach.[2] Giraldus Cambrensis tells of flesh made visible.[3] This particular miracle is continually implied in the Grail stories by the presence of the lance which wounded the side of Christ and from which the blood drips into the chalice. In the *Queste* an angel acolyte holds the lance over the cup, then Joseph takes the lance, covers the Grail with a cloth, and begins "as it were the sacrament of the mass."[4] In the *Perlesvaus* Gawain, before the Grail, sees three drops of blood fall on the altar.

[1] Cf. Dom Leclercq, *Cath. Enc.*, Art. *Host*.

[2] *Dialogus Miraculorum*, Bk. IX.

[3] *Gemma Ecclesiastica*, I: xi.

[4] The piercing of the host with a small lance has a place in Greek ritual; cf. Peebles, *Legend of Longinus*, pp. 62 ff. The same symbolic bleeding of the host into the chalice is implied in this verse of Hildebert of Lavardin:

> Ista sacramenta modio vario ponuntur in ara;
> Oblati panis dextra tenet calicem,
> In cruce pendentis quoniam latus Omnipotentis
> Dextrum sanguineam vulnere fudit aquam.
> Sic super altare litat hoc memorando sacerdos
> Hostia sicque jugis scelera nostra lavat.
> — *Versus de Mysterio Missæ, Migne*, CLXXI: 1180.

Of course miracles of this type tend to become confused with the special cult of the holy blood (*Saint Sang*), which is thereby brought directly into association with the consecration of the mass and the literal transformation of the wine into blood. Fécamp claimed not only a miracle of the bleeding host type but also the possession of a portion of the dried and clotted blood from the wounds of Christ, concealed by Nicodemus in his glove.[1] But it must be said that early pictures illustrating the *Saint Sang* cult depict the blood of Christ flowing as a fountain opened for sin and for uncleanness rather than as the source of a lifegiving drink.[2] The sensitive soul of Hugh of St. Victor shrank from these crude aids to faith though he did not deny them.[3]

To another class of these miracles belongs the appearance of a lamb or of a child on the altar, or of the Virgin holding the Christ child. Paschasius Radbertus (d. 860), already mentioned[4] as an early champion of substantial transformation of the host, records the experience of one Plecgils, who longing to be shown the exact nature of the sacramental presence of Christ, not from lack of faith, but from piety of soul, found his prayer granted. At the mass the venerable priest lifted his face and saw the Son of the Father as the infant whom Simeon was permitted to hold in his arms. Plecgils took the child into his own arms, which were trembling, and pressed his breast against the breast of Christ. He gave a kiss to God and pressed his lips against those of

[1] Some reminiscence of this relic occurs in the *Perlesvaus* (XVIII: iv), for we are told that Joseph of Arimathea had caused some of the blood of Christ to be sealed in the boss of Perceval's shield.

[2] Cf. Mâle, *L'art religieux de la fin du moyen âge en France*, II: pt. v.

[3] "In specie carnis et sanguinis non sumitur, ne humanus animus abhorreret, et sensus sibi insolita expavescerat, ut quando, orante beato Gregorio, digitus auricularis cruentatus sanguine in calice inventus ac ostensus." — *Speculum Ecclesiæ, Migne*, CLXXVII: 362.

[4] p. 15.

Christ. These things done, he restored the glorious members of the Son of God to the altar and filled the holy table with the heavenly food of Christ.[1] Similar instances are recorded by Durandus [2] and in the life of St. Hugh of Lincoln.[3] Giraldus Cambrensis speaks of a lamb or of a child in the hands of the officiating priest.[4] A chronicler of Glastonbury gravely states that Arthur was present at one such miracle.[5]

This particular kind of miracle is frequently mentioned in the Grail romances. It occurs in connection with the appearance of the Grail itself and also at the elevation of the host where no special mention of the Grail is made.[6] It is the manifestation which particularly impressed Tennyson:

> the fiery face as of a child
> That smote itself into the bread and went.

In the *Gr. St. Graal* at the communion administered by angels the host seemed to enter each mouth as a child complete in form. In the *Queste* Galahad sees a host put into the Grail and at the elevation the figure of a child descends from heaven, and all saw that the bread had the form of "dome carnel." In *Perlesvaus* it is Gawain who is favored, and it seems to him that in the midst of the Grail he sees the figure of a child.[7]

A far less significant marvel, but one worth noting in

[1] *De corpore et sanguine Domini, Migne,* CXX: 1319, 1320.

[2] *Liber de corpore et sanguine Christi,* VIII: xxviii. *Migne,* CXLIX: 1418.

[3] *Migne,* CLIII: 1036.

[4] *Gemma Ecclesiastica,* I: xi. A figure in a MS. in the Bibliotheque Nationale shows the miracle. *Vide* Rohault de Fleury, *op. cit.,* plate XXII. Illustration, p. 63.

[5] *John of Glastonbury,* ed. Hearne, I: 79. *Vide App.,* p. 126.

[6] In *Perlesvaus* (I: vi) Arthur attends mass in St. Augustine's chapel, where he sees the Virgin offer her child to the priest who places Him on the altar and goes on with the mass.

[7] VI: xix.

connection with all the rest, is the luminosity sometimes attributed to the host. Cæsarius of Heisterbach [1] tells of a holy virgin who, standing behind the priest at the elevation, saw the host in gleaming light as it were of crystal penetrated with the rays of the sun. Giraldus Cambrensis tells of a woman who by accident caught a fragment of the host in the hood of her cloak. Waking in the night she saw a luminous spot in the garment, a phenomenon also visible to her husband. This happened for three nights, when investigation revealed the host which left a spot of blood on the place it had occupied.[2] It will be remembered that in *Crestien* the Grail shines and puts out the light of the candles as the sun does that of the stars, and that de Borron [3] speaks of the great light which streams from the holy vessel carried by Christ. In *Wauchier* Perceval sees the great light in the forest made by the passing of the Grail, and in *Perlesvaus* [4] the flame of the Holy Spirit descends each day on the Grail.

One of the most interesting of the eucharistic miracles is that called by Mâle the Christ of St. Gregory.[5] This concerns a vision said to have been vouchsafed to St. Gregory as he celebrated mass in a chapel of the church of Santa Croce in Gerusalemme in Rome. The story is a shaky one, not found, according to Mâle, even in the *Legenda Aurea*. The pictures of it show St. Gregory before the altar and above it a figure of Christ either halfway in His tomb, or upright with a cross behind Him. He is thorn-crowned, and sometimes blood flows from His wounds into the chalice. This figure of Christ, alone, or with supporting angels, was later immensely popular, because an indulgence was supposed to have been granted to St. Gregory to be bestowed on those who would contemplate

---

[1] *Op. cit.*, IX: xxxiii, xxxiv.
[2] *Gemma*, I: xi.
[3] *Metr. Jos.*, ll. 718 ff.
[4] VI: xiv.
[5] *Op. cit.*, II, pt. iv.

the suffering Christ of his vision. This indulgence accounts for the numerous instances of this Christ of St. Gregory in art; it is an especial favorite as the central figure of a predella. But earlier than any date given by Mâle for a picture of the figure we find it connected with the Grail. In *Gr. St. Graal* Josephe, looking into the ark of the Grail, saw a man crucified on the cross which was held by angels, while the nails which another angel had held were in his feet and hands. The lance which had been carried by three angels was in the side of the crucified man and from it flowed a stream which was neither of blood nor of water but of the two mingled.[1] In the *Queste* a figure rises from the Grail after mass, a man who had blood-stained hands and feet and body.[2] In *Perlesvaus*[3] Gawain looks up and "it seemeth him to be the Greal all in flesh, and he seeth above, as him thinketh, a King crowned, nailed upon the Rood and the spear was still fast in His side."[4]

An entirely different group of miracles involves the reverence due the holy mysteries. The doctrine of transubstantiation and the consequent emphasis on the need of celibate purity on the part of the celebrating priest were illustrated by miracles in which the unworthy priest, presuming to say mass, finds a blast of wind overturning a chalice or the host snatched from his hands. . Such a miracle is recorded by Giraldus Cambrensis. A priest took advantage of the festivities of Christmas to complete an intrigue, going straight from it to celebrate the three masses of Christmas. To his dismay he found that at the first one the host vanished at the elevation. He pretended to complete the mass, but when the same thing happened at his other two masses he confessed his sin. After a long penance he was

---

[1] *Vide* App. 127   [2] *Vide* App. 127
[3] VI: xx. *Vide* App. 127
[4] Tr. Evans. Cf. Görres, *Die Christliche Mystik*, II: 107 f. for an account of this vision as seen by several persons at Douay.

allowed to resume his priestly functions, and lo, at his first consecration he found he had four hosts instead of one.[1] Another story with a similar moral is related by Giraldus.[2]

These miracles have their parallels in the Grail legends. In *Gr. St. Graal* Nasciens is blinded for daring to lift the cover of the Grail and see what no mortal eyes ought to behold. In the *Queste* Lancelot, at mass where the Grail is, sees that at the elevation the priest is overcome by the weight of the host. Lancelot rashly proffers aid and is struck dumb by a fiery wind.[3]

The beneficent effects of the Grail may be classed with the miracles. The Grail was agreeable to all who saw it, and the devil may not lead any man astray on the day he sees it.[4] It separates the good from the bad. It supports

---

[1] *Spec. Ec.*, IV: xxvii.

[2] *Gemma Ec.*, II: xvi. This is short and deserves to be quoted in the original. "Item magnus Basilius quotiens corpus dominicum consecrabat, columba sacramentum dominici corporis continens, quæ super altare perpendit, ipsa conversionis hora se ter in circuitu movere solebat. Quadam autem die, ipso consecrante, eamque non moveri ut solet intuente secum admirari et contristari. Statim autem in spiritu vidit diaconum, ei ad altare ministrantem, in mulierem quandam in ipso presbyterio petulanter oculos injecisse. Quo remoto, officioque suspenso, mulieribus quoque abinde remotis, Sancti Spiritus adventum per columbæ motum, ut solet, vir sanctus advertit." *Vide* illustration, p. 62.

[3] These, of course, recall incidents from the Old Testament, and it is interesting to find Giraldus (*Gemma Ec.*, I: li) using the latter to illustrate the reverence due *corpus domini*. "Item, si Oza, quia manum extenderat ad archam figuralem ne declineret bobus recalcitrantibus a Domino ad mortem percussus est, quanto magis percuti timeat a Domino qui indigne veram archam, scilicet corpus Domini, conficit vel consumit. Ille tamen ex debito officio, quia de Levi erat et sacerdos, ad sublevandum archam, sed indigne; tradunt enim Hebraei, quia nocte præcedente concuberant cum uxore. Quanto magis autem punientur accidentes ad corpus Christi concubinarium vel meretricum ne enormioris immunditiæ mentio fiat, concubitores."

[4] *Wauchier.*

Joseph in prison and feeds his starving followers. At a banquet it serves the company with such food as each prefers.

Some commentators have considered this property of producing food a hopelessly heathen survival, totally inconsistent with any feature of the eucharist. But so far from this being the case it is quite possible that this property of the magic vessel is precisely the one which recommended the story to those who combined it with that of Joseph of Arimathea. There is no more common figure of the eucharist than the miraculously produced manna. First used in the discourse of Christ Himself, [1] it is found in all Christian literature, and in *Perlesvaus* we are told that the manna fed each man with that which he most desired.[2] The catacomb representations of the eucharist are also connected with the miraculous increase of food and drink — the miracle of the loaves and fishes and the miracle of Cana.[3] Moreover, the miracle of sustaining life on the host alone is recorded in the life of many saints.[4]

These beneficent effects of the Grail are allegorical expressions of the numerous gifts and graces of the eucharist, which not only preserved body and soul to everlasting life, but was a medicine in sickness and a defence against all wiles of enemies, visible and invisible.

---

[1] St. John., VI: 49, 50.

[2] XVIII: xv. "Il les mist XL anz el désert où onques dras ne lor porri, et il lor envéoit la mainne del ciel qui lor servoit quanqu'il vouloient boivre ne mangier." Cf. Algerus, *De Sacramento*, I: xv, *Migne*, CLXXX: 786.

[3] *Vide* illustration, p. 63.

[4] Cf. Cæsarius of Heisterbach, *op. cit.*, IX: xlvi.

XII

Is this marked resemblance between the characteristics of the Grail and its miracles and those of transubstantiation accidental? Or is it rather that the point to be demonstrated is one and the same, namely the literal and miraculous presence of God on the altar? All these miracles are connected with the vision of God in the eucharist, and their object is to give aid and comfort to those who need sight to sustain their faith. They are visions, it is true, and signs of the favorable mercy of God. But more blessed than even the witnesses of a transubstantiation miracle are those who like Catherine of Siena taste and see the whole mystery of the Trinity in their eucharistic rapture.

As we should expect, it is in the *Queste* that this spiritualized vision is most clearly expressed. We find there both the agony of the knight who fails to attain it, and the rapture of him to whom it is granted. Bohort, whose quest of the Grail is hindered by his one sin against purity, seeks consolation from a hermit who hears his confession, absolves him, and prepares to administer the eucharist to him. After the consecration he takes *corpus domini* and signs Bohort to come forward. And when he had kneeled before him, the good man said, "Bohort, do you see what I hold?" "Sir," said he, "I see that you hold my Saviour and my redemption in form of bread, and in such fashion have I ever seen it. But my eyes are so earthly that they cannot discern spiritual things, nor do they let me see otherwise than to deprive me of the sight of the true form. For I have never doubted that it is truly flesh and truly man and God." And he commenced to weep bitterly. There is no flaw in his faith, the hermit does not refuse him the communion, but the mystic vision of God in the eucharist is withheld from him.

Very different is the experience of Galahad. He has been vouchsafed the eucharistic miracles, has seen the child on the altar and the Christ of St. Gregory, but a greater thing is in store for him, the full revelation of the Grail. Joseph of Arimathea appears and celebrates a mass. At the consecration (*el secre de la messe*) he lifts the paten from the holy vessel and bids Galahad look within. Galahad comes forward, just as Bohort had done, but looking within he trembles as does mortal flesh when it beholds spiritual things — "esperitels choses," the very words used by Bohort to describe that which was hidden from him. Then Galahad stretched his hands to heaven and said: "Lord, I thank Thee that Thou hast granted my wish. For now I see plainly that which tongue cannot speak nor heart think. Thou hast granted me to see what I have so long desired."

After this he, like Bohort, meekly and gladly receives the Lord's body. But where Bohort had rested on faith alone, to Galahad has come mystic certainty of the eucharistic presence of Christ wrought by the miracle of transubstantiation. He sees the marvels of the Grail; the quest is achieved.[1]

[1] For the full text of these two passages in the *Queste* see App., p. 127. This conception of the Grail as the symbol of the miracle of transubstantiation, consummate gift of divine love, is found in a German poem published in *Meisterlieder der Kolmarer handschrift*, ed. Bartsch, p. 592. It is addressed to four who know the true meaning of love, — lady, knight, poet, and priest. The last is told of his high privilege in being permitted to hold in his own hands the Grail of the love of the King of kings.

> Ach priester, wer möht überkomen
> die zale dîner hôhen wirde gar:
> al zifferîe kraft möht ez niht halp besinnen zwâr.
> Du hast vil schône an dich genomen
> ein sîdîn kleit, dar in bris ich dich eben,
> sît dirz der hœchste fürst von himel ze êren hât gegeben.
> Wart daz duz iht beselwest durch daz wunder,

sît got ûf dich geworfen hât besunder
reines lobes zunder,
lâ brinnen schiezen dich der minnen grâl
des hœhsten küngs der sich lât schowen in dîner hende sal.

For this and other references to the use of the word "grail" in German poetry I am indebted to Hertz, *Parzival*, p. 459. The inferences I have drawn from them are entirely my own.

Since this chapter went to press, the following statement, most interesting in this connection, came to my notice. According to Peter Calo, his earliest biographer, Aquinas, before receiving the viaticum, made this declaration:

"Si major scientia, quam fides de hoc sacramento in hac vita haberi potest, in illa respondeo, quod vere credo et pro certo scio, hunc deum verum esse et hominem, dei patris et virginis matris filium et sic credo animo et confiteor verbo."

For this citation from Calo's *Vita*, (put forth c. 1300 and included in *Fontes Vitæ S. Thomæ Aquinatis*, ed. Prümmer), I am indebted to the painstaking courtesy of the Rev. D. J. Kennedy, O. P., Dominican House of Studies, Washington, D. C.

THE MYSTIC VISION IN THE *DIVINE COMEDY*

Jesu, quem velatum nunc aspicio,
Oro, fiat illud quod tam sitio
Ut, te revelata cernens facie,
Visu sim beatus tuæ gloriæ.
—Thomas Aquinas

THE MYSTIC VISION IN THE *DIVINE COMEDY*

WHEN we come to the consideration of the eucharistic influence in the *Divine Comedy* we are conscious of a very different atmosphere from that of the Grail romances, and the difference is not merely a matter of literary expression, but also of devotional mood. The romantic treatment is not only chronologically much nearer the first emphatically material statements of transubstantiation, but it represents the secular reaction to them; it records popular piety with its crudely literal acceptance of the miracle and its occasional glimpse of the spiritual thing. The romance writers, though they might possess a saving acquaintance with the teaching of the church, cannot be supposed to have either known or cared much about the arguments which supported any article of faith. If we find theological propositions here and there we are likely to consider them traces of a monkish original, or to suspect that they were inserted at the request of an ecclesiastical patron.

But Dante is not only a conscious literary artist, accepting or rejecting material as it is or is not adapted to his highly organized and carefully balanced structure, but an expert theologian as well, incapable of treating casually or crudely any part of the divine science. Moreover, theological discourse itself had undergone changes in the course of a century, and the schoolmen, by formulating and emphasizing the distinction between substance and accidents, had done much to modify the startling materialism of the earlier statements of transubstantiation, explaining that though the "substance," or reality, of the consecrated bread and wine was that of the body and blood of Christ, yet their "accidents," or characteristic properties — taste, smell, color, and the like — remained. From Dante, as their pupil, we should therefore expect a more spiritual as well as a more carefully organized handling of eucharistic teaching than any of which the romancers were capable.

II

It is, indeed, difficult to conceive how Dante in his great epic of the soul in its relation to God could have ignored the eucharistic doctrine and devotion so intimately connected with Christian living, albeit we should expect to find so spiritual a theme veiled under one of the "mystic senses" of the allegory. Though the subject of the *Divine Comedy* may be "the state of souls after death," the end of it is "to remove those living *in this life* from the state of misery and lead them to the state of felicity," [1] and with this end in view it would be hardly possible for him to omit all reference to the sacramental means afforded by the church for reaching the goal.

In its ultimate form this state of felicity is neither more nor less than the *visio Dei*, the complete illumination of the soul:

> Then shall be seen that which we hold by faith,
> Not demonstrated, but known of itself,
> Like to the primal truth that man believes.[2]

This immediate knowledge of God, which in its fulness comes to man only as his final reward, is always enjoyed by the angels:

---

[1] *Ep. to Can Grande.*
[2] "Lì si vedrà ciò che tenem per fede,
Non dimostrato, ma fia per sè noto,
A guisa del ver primo che l'uom crede."
Par. II: 43–45.

Every essence and virtue proceeds from the primal one and the lower intelligences receive it as from a radiating source, and throw the rays of their superior upon these inferior, after the fashion of mirrors.[1]

But though in this life man may hope only for partial attainment of knowledge, though his mirrors may give but shadowy reflection,[2] some foretaste of the state of felicity is always possible. Whence, then, is such partial knowledge, where are mirrors to be found? The answer is given at length in the work of Dionysius, from which Dante derived his ideas of angelic illumination.[3] As has been said, Dionysius follows his treatise on the angelic ranks by one on the church and its orders, showing that in the church are to be found the means whereby man attains to some share in this illumination and that these means are identical with the sacraments. In other words, the sacraments are the clouded mirrors which so modify the intensity of the divine splendor that man may look thereon and still live.

III

But just because they are at best but clouded mirrors, means adapted to powers as yet imperfect, sacraments belong to this life, they are part of the equipment of the church on earth,[4] and Dante could treat of them only in

---

[1] *Ep. to Can Grande.*

[2] "Videmus nunc per speculum in enigmate: tunc autem facie ad faciem: nunc cognosco ex parte: tunc autem cognoscam sicut et cognitus sum." *1. Cor.* xiii: 12.

[3] *Ep. to Can Grande.*

[4] "Quia ergo hoc sacramento non est in æternum mors Christi annuntianda, sed tantum donec veniat, qui postea nullis mysteriis egebimus, constat illud transitorium esse signum et temporale, quo tantum egemus nunc, dum videmus per speculum et in enigmate." — Algerus, *De Sacramento* 1: VIII, *Migne,* CLXXX: 764.

that part of the *Divine Comedy* wherein the church militant,
so to speak, has jurisdiction — the *Purgatory*. The souls
in Hell are permanently excommunicate, and those in Paradise are already included in the church triumphant; but
those who are in process of purification share in the benefits
of the ordinances of religion. Every reader must have expe-
rienced the sensation of breathing more freely in the *Purgatory*, of moving within the limits of mortal experience and
aspiration. It has a far more intimate application to the
spiritual life of the average human being, conscious of the
closeness of grandeur to the dust, than either the dreary
hoplessness of Hell or the enraptured bliss of Heaven. The
souls there, like ourselves, are still striving to leave the lower
and mount upward, still burdened with shortcomings, still
needing to join in the universal human cry, "Miserere mei,
Domine!" The essential difference between their state and
ours is, of course, their certainty of ultimate salvation, a
certainty never attained until death has ended man's pro-
bation; but this difference is only borne in on us now and
again, notably in the eleventh canto where the souls explain
that though they still say, "Lead us not into temptation,"
the prayer is for the living, they themselves need it no
longer.[1] But though free from temptation, the souls in
Purgatory have but partial knowledge of God; they must
still content themselves with seeing in a glass darkly, still
avail themselves of the means of grace. It is noticeable that
Dante introduces all through the *Purgatory* allusions more
or less definite to the scriptural phrases, the hymns, the
liturgy and sacraments which are the outward expression
of the spiritual life.[2]

---

[1] XI: 22–24.

[2] In the *Purgatory* these vary in character, sounding the whole
gamut of Christian experience: those in the *Paradise* (as in III: 121,
122; VII: 1–3, XXIII: 128, XXIV: 113, XXV: 98) express faith,
trust, and, above all, praise.

The psalm of Israel's deliverance is the song of those crossing the sea to begin the work of making themselves fair,[1] and in accordance with the religious experience of the ages it is also in the words of the psalms that abasement,[2] holy joy,[3] and trust find expression.[4] Hymns from the Breviary sound in the flowery valley [5] and in the last circle.[6] The successful passage through the gate of Purgatory is marked, as are earthly conquests, by *Te Deum laudamus*,[7] and the triumph of Purgatory in the release of a soul to its full attainment of the benefits of the Incarnation can find no more fitting utterance than that which hailed the first tidings of the Word made flesh, *Gloria in excelsis Deo*.[8]

Nor is the sacramental system unnoticed. Though embraced by the arms of infinite love, Manfred must pay the penalty of dying without the last sacraments and spend thirty times the period of his contumacy in Antepurgatory before his ascent to purification may begin.[9] At the gate of Purgatory itself there is an angel, guardian of the entrance as far as the narrative goes, but standing also for the ecclesiastical hierarchy whose representative may, by the power of the keys, bind and loose. Next come the three steps signifying the contrition, confession, and satisfaction without which no one can attain the purity of heart necessary for either sacramental union here or for the ultimate oneness with God. The seven P's marked by the angel on Dante's forehead, which must be erased one by one at the end of each toilsome climb, stand not only for the seven mortal sins but also for the penance imposed, which must be accomplished before further sacramental grace may be received.[10] But it is in that part of the *Purgatory* which Dante has

---

[1] *Purg.* II: 46.
[2] *Ib.* XIX: 73.
[3] *Ib.* XXVIII: 80.
[4] *Ib.* XXX: 83, 84.
[5] *Ib.* VIII: 13.
[6] *Ib.* XXV: 121.
[7] *Ib.* IX: 140.
[8] *Ib.* XX: 136.
[9] *Ib.* III: 136–141.
[10] *Ib.* IX: 76 ff.

set in the Earthly Paradise that we should expect the most
complete figuring of the system, for sacraments are weapons
of the church militant, and the Earthly Paradise, the literal Eden, which was supposed to exist somewhere in the
far East, is very commonly considered as a symbol of the
church. The river issuing from it is taken by Isidor of
Seville to symbolize baptism [1] and the fruit of its tree of
life, according to Hugh of St. Victor, is a type of the
eucharist.[2] And it is there, in fact, that he witnesses a
procession, the features and implications of which bear
marked resemblance to the procession of Corpus Christi
day, which at the time the *Purgatory* was written, had but
lately been advanced from a matter of tradition and custom to one of official authorization. There, too, he is sub-
merged in a flowing river that his purification may be
effected.

IV

Marked developments in eucharistic worship took place
between the Lateran Council of 1215 and the early fourteenth century, and these developments undoubtedly had
their effect on certain details in Dante's treatment of the
matter. The council's final and authoritative statement of
eucharistic doctrine had the effect of stimulating the elaboration of eucharistic ritual which had been growing up
during the preceding century, especially that which centred
in the actual moment of consecration and the elevation of
the host announced by the sacring bell. But one honor to
the eucharist was lacking — a day of festal celebration

[1] *Mysticorum Expositiones Sacramentorum, seu Quœstiones in vetus
Testamentum. In Genesin, Cap. III: 2, Migne,* LXXXIII: 216. For
text *vide* App. p. 136. Cf. the source of the waters of the Earthly
Paradise, *Purg.* XXVIII: 124 ff., and the use made of these waters,
Ib. XXXI: 91–102.

[2] *Vide ut inf.,* p. 114.

specially devoted to it. Maunday Thursday, the day of its institution, though called both *Cœna Domini* and *Natalis Calicis*, was too deeply shadowed by Christ's passion to be a fitting occasion for rejoicing.

It was in the Low Countries that the first attempt to meet this need was made. Julianna, prioress of Mont-Corneillon near Liège, had a vision in which she saw the full moon disfigured by a black spot. This she interpreted as meaning that the black spot on the church calendar was the want of a day devoted to the honor of the sacrament of the altar. The idea became popular in Liège, and the bishop, Robert de Tarote, authorized the local celebration of the festival. In 1261 the archdeacon of Liège, Jacob Pantaleon, became Pope under the title of Urban IV. He wished to give full sanction to the new feast, but hesitated about the final step, it is said, until his decision was quickened by a miracle of the bleeding host, known as the miracle of Bolsena. In 1264 he issued the bull *Transiturus*, establishing the festival of Corpus Christi, to be held on the Thursday succeeding Trinity Sunday. The bull declared the object of the celebration to be the strengthening and exaltation of the Catholic faith, and its keynote was festivity. Devout throngs of the faithful were to betake themselves to the churches, and the clergy as well as the rejoicing laity were to raise the song of praise. With heart and mouth all were to hymn the joy of salvation. Faith was bidden to sing psalms, hope to dance joyfully, and charity to exult. Devotion was to add its plaudits, the choir to hold jubilee, purity to rejoice. Fulfilling their devout purpose worthily, all should unite in celebrating the solemnity of the day.[1]

---

[1] "Nos itaque ad corroborationem et exaltationem catholicæ fidei, digne ac rationabiliter duximus statuendum, ut de tanto Sacramento præter quotidianam memoriam, quam de ipso facit Ecclesia, solemnior et specialior annuatim memoria celebretur, certum ad hoc designantes et describentes diem, videlicet feriam quintam proximam post octavam

It is told that Urban requested both Thomas Aquinas and Bonaventura to draw up an office for the day. When the time came for reading them, each wished the other to begin. St. Thomas consented to be first, but when it came Bonaventura's turn he smilingly shook from the loose sleeve of his habit a shower of bits of paper. He had realized as the reading proceeded that there could be no question of choice and so had spared the Pope the onus of decision.[1] And indeed it would be hard to conceive of an improvement on the work of Aquinas with its skilful use of type and antitype, its aptness of scriptural adaptation, and its superb eucharistic hymns: *Pange lingua, Sacris solemniis juncta sunt gaudia, Lauda Sion, Verbum supernum prodiens.* Part of this last, *O salutaris hostia,* is perhaps best known of all eucharistic hymns.

V

Neither in this office nor in the bull of Urban is there any mention of the procession which became the most striking feature of the celebration, and there has been much dispute and uncertainty as to just when it was instituted. It seems to have been officially authorized only at the council of Vienne, 1311, but Roman Catholic writers generally agree

Pentecostes, ut in ipsa quinta feria devotæ turbæ fidelium propter hoc ad Ecclesias affectuosæ concurrant, et tam clerici, quam populi gaudentes, in cantica laudum surgant. Tunc enim omnium corda et vota, ora et labia, hymnos persolvant lætitiæ salutaris; tunc psallat fides; spes tripudiet; exultet charitas; devotio plaudat; jubilet chorus; puritas jucundetur. Tunc singuli, alacri animo, pronaque voluntate conveniant sua studia laudabiliter exequendo, tanti festi solemnitatem celebrantes. Et utinam ad Christi servitium sic eius fideles ardor inflammet, ut per hæc et alia proficientibus ipsis meritorum cumulis apud eum, qui sese dedit pro eis in pretium, tribuitque se ipsis in pabulum, tandem post huius vitæ decursum eis se in præmium largiatur." — *Bullarum Romanum,* ed. Taurinensis, III: 707.

[1] Cf. Eugène Cortet, *Essai sur les fêtes religieuses,* 1867.

that this authorization was rather the sanction of a custom already established than the inauguration of a new one. According to Martène contemporary books of ritual show that the procession followed very closely on the institution of the festival.[1] Catalani goes further and declares the consensus of opinion is that Urban was the "author" of the procession as well as of the bull. His first argument for this opinion is the intrinsic one, namely, that the bull requires a measure of rejoicing, "tripudatio, exultatio et jubilatio," which being entirely out of keeping with the celebration of mass in church, necessarily implies an outdoor procession, and he contends, moreover, that only by the transportation of the most holy sacrament through the highways could be illustrated that triumph of Christ over the perfidy and madness of heretics which Urban declared to be one object of the festival. In the second place he considers the conclusions of writers who have made a special study of the period and who believe almost unanimously that the procession coincided, nearly if not precisely, with the first observation of the day. His third point is that the procession of Corpus Christi day was an elaboration rather than an innovation.[2] There is plenty of evidence for this.

The mediæval popes were accustomed to have the host carried before them on journeys and state occasions,[3] and the viaticum was carried to the sick in a procession with lights and bells.[4] That the host was a central figure in processions of intercession appears in Geoffrey of Monmouth's account of the Scottish prelates who with all their clergy in attendance came out to beg mercy from King

[1] *Ec. rit.* IV: xxix.

[2] *Pont. Rom:* II: 311 ff. For text see App. p. 128.

[3] Cf. Catalani, *op. cit.* II: 313; Picart, *Cérémonies et coutumes religieuses*, Art. *Corpus Christi*.

[4] Cf. Wilkins, *Consilia Magnæ Britannicæ et Hiberniæ*, I: 623. Stone, *op. cit.* I: 352 ff.

Arthur, bearing the relics of the saints and the sacraments of the church.[1] This practice also obtained in Provence.[2] A similar instance in the romance of *Perlesvaus* has already been noted.[3] To judge from their records the custom must have been favored by the Normans, and Lanfranc, as became an opponent of Berengar, took care to provide for so edifying and instructive a ceremony in England. In his *Decreti pro ordine S. Benedicti*[4] he gives elaborate directions for the procession on Palm Sunday. The green things were to be blessed and distributed, the palms to ecclesiastics and persons of importance; flowers and leaves to the rest. The procession included not only the officiating clergy but the monks, the boys with their master, and the friars. They advanced, two by two, accompanied by banners, crucifixes, lighted candles, censers, and two subdeacons carrying texts of the gospels. Singing as they went, they left the church and took up a station outside. Two priests then left the procession and went back into the church for the *feretrum*,[5] which had been prepared by the same priests at earliest dawn and in which the body of Christ was hidden. When they returned to the station they took up their stand on either side of the *feretrum*, around which all stood in reverent ranks, the children, as befitted the day, being placed in front. At the antiphon, *Hosanna, filio David, benedictus qui venit in nomine Domini, Hosanna in excelsis*, all bowed the knee.

---

[1] "Convenerunt omnes Episcopi miserandæ patriæ, cum omni clero sibi subdito, reliquias sanctorum et ecclesiastica sacramenta nudis ferentes pedibus." *Historia regum Britanniæ* ed. San Marte, IX: vi.

[2] "His gestis, episcopus Tolosæ qui erat in exercitu, mandavit præposito ecclesiæ aliisque clericis ut de civitate Tolosana egrederentur; qui statim jussa complentes, nudibus Pedibus cum corpore Christi egressi sunt Tolosa."
Petrus Sarnensis, *Historia Albigensium*, LV. *Migne*, CCXIII: 611.

[3] *Vide ut sup.*, p. 29.

[4] *Migne*, CL: 455 ff. For text *vide*. App. p. 129.

[5] "Pyx in qua cœna Eucharistia conditur." Du Cange.

Then to another antiphon, *Ave, rex noster,* the bearers of the *feretrum* took up their burden, and the procession went on through the city, the people bending the knee as the host passed in front of them. This custom was not confined to the Normans.[1] Also in various places on Good Friday the host, instead of a crucifix, was interred in the Easter Sepulchre, from which it was carried with much pomp and ceremony on Easter morning.[2]

Processions centering around the host were, then, already established by the middle of the thirteenth century, and, very naturally, were early adapted to the Corpus Christi celebration. As this feature gradually became the characteristic part of the ceremonies of the day, other eucharistic processions seem to have been largely discontinued in its favor. Civil and ecclesiastical authorities united in the celebration, and the route of the procession was often a long one. The bells of all churches in front of which it passed were rung as well as that of the chief church of the city from which it started. The streets were carefully cleaned in preparation and tapestries were hung from the windows.[3] As in the earlier processions there were always lights, either candles, in huge candlesticks, or lanterns. Whether directly from the association with Palm Sunday, or indirectly from the very ancient custom of strewing flowers and boughs before a conqueror, flowers became, and have remained, a marked feature of the procession. The houses along the route were

[1] Cf. *Migne,* LXXXV: 391n.

[2] On Easter morning the two oldest priests went to the sepulchre "out of the which . . they tooke a marvelous beautiful Image of our Saviour, representing the resurrection, with a crosse in his hand, in the breast whereof was enclosed in bright christall the holy Sacrament of the altar through which christall the blessed host was conspicuous to the behoulders." — *Ancient Monuments, Rites and Customs of Durham, Surtees Society Publications,* XV: 10, 11. Cf. also Stone, *op. cit.* I: 385 for such processions at Salisbury, Hereford, York and Canterbury.

[3] Cf. Picart, *op. cit.*

decorated with green boughs, and sometimes, as at Genzano in the Alban hills, the flowers were woven into an elaborate carpet for the main street.

In the midst of the procession a baldachino was carried; sometimes the bearers were priests, sometimes laymen, but always crowned with flowers.[1] Underneath this, one or more of the officiating ecclesiastics bore the host, while before it boys with garlands on their heads scattered rose leaves, and members of guilds and the populace followed all carrying tapers. Sometimes the little St. John Baptist was the immediate predecessor of the canopy, and the patron saints of the city and its trades were represented by persons dressed in appropriate costumes.

It is easy to understand that under the influence of the guilds these figures increased in number and became performers in the miracle cycles.[2] The celebration of the day tended to become more formal and elaborate, and culminated in the Spanish *autos sacramentales*, which found their greatest exponent in Calderon. Still, religious customs change very slowly; there is not much difference between the ordinary Corpus Christi processions of the nineteenth century and those described in Reformation satire, and the latter probably included much that came unchanged from the beginnings three centuries earlier. It may, therefore, be worth while to refer to Kirchmaier's scornful enumeration

[1] Martène speaks of a miniature which shows clergy and laity crowned with flowers. "Idem eruiter ex missale Melodunensi, in quo feria 5, post festum SS. Trinitatis habetur missa de SS. Sacramento, cui appicta est imago sacerdotis sacram eucharistiam manu gestantis, sub baldachino a quatuor viris delato, qui perinde ac sacerdos ipse reliquique clerici nudum caput florum coronis ornatum habent." — *op. cit.* IV: xxix, 5 (ed. 1764).

[2] Lydgate, in the *Procession of Corpus Christi*, (early fifteenth century), first summons patriarchs and prophets to the festival, giving a stanza to the teaching of each viewed in connection with the eucharist. Next he takes up the New Testament characters, in the same way; then the fathers, ending with Thomas Aquinas.

of the details of one, with its flowers, lights, and allegorical figures.[1]

[1] "Then doth ensue the solemne feast of *Corpus Christi day*.
Who then can shewe their wicked vse, and fonde and foolish play?
The hallowed bread with worship great, in siluer Pix they beare
About the Church, or in the Citie passing here and theare.
His armes that beares the same, two of the welthiest men do holde,
And over him a Canopey of silke and cloth of golde.

. . . .

Christes passion here derided is, with sundrie maskes and playes,
Fair Ursley with hir maydens all, doth passe amid the wayes:
And valiant George, with speare thou killest the dreadfull dragon
here:
The deuils house is drawne about, wherein there doth appere
A wondrous sort of damned sprites, with foule and fearefull looke;
Great Christopher doth wade and passe with Christ amid the
brooke;
Sebastian full of feathred shaftes, the dint of dart doth feele,
There walketh Kathren with her sworde in hande, and cruell
wheele:
The Challis and the singing Cake, with Barbara is led,
And sundrie other Pageants playde in worship of this bred,
That please the foolish people well: what shoulde I stand vpon,
Their Banners, Crosses, Candlestickes, and reliques many on,
Their Cuppes and carued Images, that priestes with countnance hie,
Or rude and common people beare about full solemlie?
Saint John before the bread doth go, and poynting towardes him,
Doth shew the same to be the Lambe that takes away our sinne:
On whome two clad in Angels shape do sundrie flowres fling,
A number great of sacring Belles, with pleasant sounde doering.
The common wayes with bowes are strawde, and every streete
beside,
An to the walles and windowes all, are boughes and braunches tide.
The Monkes in every place do roame, the Nonnes abrode are sent,
The Priestes and schoolemen lowde do rore, some vse the instru-
ment.
The straunger passing through the streete, vpon his knees doe fall:
And earnestly upon this bread, as on his God doth call."

Fourth Book of the Popish Kingdom, or reigne of Antichrist written in Latine verse by Thomas Naogeorgus (or Kirchmaier) and englyshed by Barnabe Googe. Anno 1570.

VI

A comparison of the Corpus Christi procession with that at the close of Dante's *Purgatory* cannot fail to bring out striking resemblances between them. These resemblances, as will be seen on close examination, involve general trend and purpose as well as detail, and it is hard to believe them purely accidental. They may therefore be considered carefully in the hope of finding in them the clew to a really convincing interpretation of the last six cantos of the *Purgatory*.

While certain features of the allegory in these cantos have been studied minutely and at great length their whole bearing has been rather casually dismissed by criticism. So Vossler, in his æsthetic interpretation of the *Divine Comedy*,[1] considers Dante's whole treatment of the Earthly Paradise a blunder with disastrous consequences, a blunder which the ideas of his age forced even upon the greatest genius.[2] Symonds thought that "to a modern taste this pageant is artistically a failure. The difficulty of identifying all the personages who play parts in it, and the dryness of the abstract imagery, overtax the attention of readers accustomed to greater freedom and directness of poetical presentation." [3] The best that is said of it is a tempered praise of its value as an example of allegory carried to its highest pitch and therefore deserving close study.[4] There has been little attempt to account for the character of the procession or for its place at the very gates of heaven. Nor has any interpretation placed the episode of the Earthly Paradise in balanced relation to the entire poem; it has been credited with no structural value.

[1] Karl Vossler, *Die Göttliche Komödie*, II: ii, pp. 238–245.

[2] "Kurz, dieser Irrtum ist der Zins, den auch das grösste Genie seinem Zeitalter zu entrichten gehalten ist." *Ib.* p. 245.

[3] *Introduction to the Study of Dante*, ch. iv.

[4] Moore, *Studies in Dante*, III: 178 ff.

On one point, however, the critics are in very general agreement, and that is that in the mystical procession Dante meant to show forth the triumph of the church universal, represented by the chariot, drawn by the two-natured griffin, symbol of Christ. There is no reason to dispute this explanation as far as it goes, even if one insists upon the eucharistic association, for one object of the feast of Corpus Christi was to show forth the triumph of the church which centred in the glorification of the eucharist. But, though the peculiarly joyous character of the episode, with it accessories of flowers, lights, and symbolic figures, might be traced directly to the ancient triumph, and need not be derived from the new festival, the explanation is inadequate, offering no solution for many obvious questions.

Why, for example, is Beatrice the central figure? It has been said that she here personifies revelation, or the authority of the church, or the ideal papacy. It is never safe, of course, to claim a single, exclusive meaning for any part of Dante's allegory, and Beatrice may figure all of these, but not one of them accounts for her sudden descent into the midst of such a procession. In any of these characters her fitting place would be within the chariot at its first appearance, but Dante becomes aware of her presence only after certain ceremonies of ritual significance.

Again, to whom are the various salutations addressed? Does "Blessed art thou among women" [1] refer to Beatrice, or is it literally a hymn to the Virgin. When the figure representing the book of *Canticles* chants, "Come forth from Lebanon, O spouse," [2] is the welcomed one the church, or is it Beatrice? Who is called blessed as coming in the name of the Lord? [3] Commentators differ and no unifying suggestion is made.

It is, therefore, worth while to make a study of the procession in the Earthly Paradise, deliberately taking as a

[1] *Purg.* XXIX: 85–87.　　[2] *Ib.* XXX: 11.　　[3] *Ib.* XXX: 19.

key its eucharistic implications, shown not only in its undeniable resemblance to that of Corpus Christi but in other ways.

VII

Dante conceives the Earthly Paradise as a plain on the top of the mount of purification and in it he places the scene of the end of the *Purgatory*. It is a place of primeval loveliness, cool shade, and gleaming water, made bright by many flowers. As he enters it, Dante, fresh from purifying pain, sees Matilda gathering the flowers as she sings the joy of the forgiven. Fearing to lose sight of her, the first soul he has encountered who has entered into the inheritance of bliss, he keeps pace with her as she moves along the far side of Lethe. At a turn of the stream they find themselves looking eastward, and, in front of them, a sudden flash of light through the forest announces a great pageant. Seven golden candlesticks, the lamps of the Spirit, move forward over the flower-strewn ground, their streaming lights typifying its sevenfold gifts.[1] Before and behind the central group, the car and the griffin, move symbolic figures which represent the books of the Bible. In the vanguard are four and twenty elders, white-robed and crowned with lilies. These represent the books of the Old Testament, and in so doing may indicate as well the introit, a part of the eucharistic liturgy.

The words of the introit are chanted as the clergy and assistants enter the choir at the beginning of mass. These words are taken almost exclusively from the Old Testament,

---

[1] There is, of course, much dispute as to the symbolism of the "sette liste" (*Purg.* XXIX: 77), and, no doubt, Dante may have had more than one significance in mind. But the seven lamps of the Spirit in the Apocalypse (*Rev.* IV: 5) are so frequently associated with the seven gifts of the Spirit (based on *Isaiah* XI: 2; cf. *Conv.* IV: xxi), that he could hardly have failed to provide a symbol for the latter.

because, according to the complicated symbolism which was worked into every part of the mass, the opening procession represented the participation of the whole church in the coming of Christ, and the words chosen to accompany it were those of the patriarchs and prophets in order that the prophetic share of the saints of the Old Dispensation in the acceptance of Christ might be commemorated.[1] So it is most fitting that the figures of those who rejoiced aforetime in the promise of Christ should hail the renewal of His coming with the supreme Salutation and promise of salvation, — "Blessed art thou among the daughters of Adam,"[2] ending with the praise of the mother of Christ. For the Salutation, first uttered, greeted the coming of Christ in the flesh, a coming perpetually renewed in the miracle of the mass.[3]

After the books of the Old Testament come the four beasts figuring the gospels, which are the records of the incarnate life of Christ, of the consummation of man's redemption, and of the eucharistic commemoration thereof. After them the two-natured griffin, figure of Christ, draws the chariot of the church.[4] This, significantly, comes between the books

[1] *Vide.* App. p. 133.

[2] *Purg.* XXIX: 85–87.

[3] The mother of Christ is frequently addressed as a vessel of the sacrament:

> "Vale urna, manna, merum,
> panem cœli portans verum."
> — *Hymni Latini*, Mone, II: 270.

> "Gaude virgo ætherea,
> uvam mitem parturiens,
> urna decens et aurea,
> verum manna suscipiens."
> — *Ib.* II: 186.

[4] Dante's acknowledged reminiscence of *Ezekiel* (*Purg.* XXIX: 100) is interesting not only on account of the four beasts but in relation to the chariot. Jewish mysticism found much of its expression in

concerned with the coming of Christ and those which record the establishment of His kingdom on earth — the church. These last, representatives of the new law, are also crowned with flowers, but blood red, like fire above their brows, for the new law is that of love, and for Dante its color is therefore that of living flame.[1] In keeping with the general Corpus Christi associations the attendant angels scatter flowers above and around, and the figures of the virtues rejoice in a festal dance.

Turning to the chariot "as to their peace," the ministers and messengers of life eternal unite in singing "Benedictus

the *Ma'aseh Merkabah,* "work of the chariot," which dealt with the visible manifestations of God. There was in some quarters a belief that certain mystic expositions of *Ezekiel* I, or even of subjects connected with it, would cause God to appear. The initiated believed themselves to enter into the heavenly chariot and in it ascend to the heavens where they saw God. Philo adopted the idea of the chariot and its charioteer, Metatron, and applied it to the *Logos.* Cf. Abelson, *Jewish Mysticism;* *Jewish Encyclopœdia,* Art. *Chariot.* This is tempting, but so far I have found nothing else to show that Dante ever heard of this particular conception of the *visio Dei.*

[1] That the relation of the prophets of the Old Testament and the saints of the New to the first coming of Christ is continued in their relation to His eucharistic presence is shown in a Corpus Christi *ludus.* (*Altdeutsche Schauspiele,* ed. Mone). It is headed "Incipit ludus utilis pro devotione simplicium intimandus et peragendus die corporis Christi vel infra octaves, de fide katholica." Beginning with Adam and Eve the Old Testament characters repeat their foretellings of Christ, and alternately the New Testament characters, John the Baptist, apostles and magi, give their experience. At the end the Pope sums it all up in the eucharist: —

> "daz wir nymmer muessen ersterben,
> wir mussen gotes hulde erwerben,
> daz uns sin heylger lychnam werde gegeben
> czü eynem geleyte in daz ewige leben.
> daz uns daz allen musse gesehen,
> dar um sö sprecht amen."

It will be noticed that this arrangement is much the same as that in Lydgate's poem referred to on p. 98.

qui venis" as they, too, scatter flowers.[1] Now these words, slightly modified, as is also the angelic salutation,[2] are the very last sung by the assistants before the canon of the mass. The *Sanctus*, which embodies the heavenly worship of the Lamb that was slain, is joined to the *Benedictus*, the worship offered on Palm Sunday to the Lamb about to be led to the slaughter.[3] The significance of the words in the liturgy is undoubtedly, that as they were first sung to welcome Christ into His city of Jerusalem, so now they greet Christ Whom the faithful expect on the altar at the words of consecration.[4] In this chant the eucharistic meaning, implicit in the character of procession, is fully unfolded.

VIII

But the heart of the Corpus Christi pageant is the host under its canopy, while here the festival centres in the veiled

[1] *Purg.* XXX: 18–20.

[2] *Ib.* XXIX: 85–87.

[3] "Sanctus, Sanctus, Sanctus, Dominus Deus Sabaoth. Pleni sunt cœli et terra gloria tua. Hosanna in excelsis. Benedictus qui venit in nomine Domini. Hosanna in excelsis."

"Post finitum hymnum: *Sanctus, Sanctus, Sanctus,* inclinant se circumstantes, venerando divinam majestatem cum angelis, et Domini incarnationem cum turbis." Hildebert of Lavardin, *Liber de expositione missæ, Migne,* CLXXI: 1161.

[4] "To the praise of the triune God follows the jubilant salutation of the Redeemer, who will soon appear mystically on the altar 'in fulness of mercy.' The hymn concludes with the triumphal chant with which the Savior was welcomed by the multitudes as Prince of Peace and conqueror of death at His solemn entrance into Jerusalem, and with which He is now again saluted at His coming on the altar. . . .

How profoundly significant is this formula of worship, this grateful and joyous praise of the Savior inserted here, at this part of the Mass, when He is on the point of re-appearing in our midst as a victim, as formerly He entered into Jerusalem to accomplish on the Cross the bloody sacrifice." Nicholas Gihr, *The Holy Sacrifice of the Mass.*, tr. St. Louis, 1902, pp. 565–567.

figure of Beatrice. She appears in its midst as suddenly and as silently as the sacramental presence of Christ comes to the altar at the words of consecration. It is for her that the lights blaze, the flowers are strewn, and the great cry of greeting and welcome goes up. She is the burden of the chariot beside which Faith, Hope, and Charity circle in a dance even as the bull of Pope Urban had required.[1] One naturally asks why Dante's lost love should return to him as the main figure of this triumph of Christian worship, enthroned within the church, hailed as is the miracle of transubstantiation, honored, as is the host, in solemn procession? Why, indeed, if not to show at the outset of her visible return that she is now and hereafter not the lost love but the mystic Beatrice, divinely appointed agent of Dante's salvation and enlightenment?

It is quite true that, even in his most earthly mood, Dante never failed to find spiritual significance in his relation to Beatrice. At his first meeting with Bice Portinari, the neighbor's little daughter, his eyes were opened and he knew something of the function and power of love. When he came to write of the experiences of his childhood and first youth in the *New Life*, discerning more clearly her meaning for him, he spoke of her as blessedness, as salvation, for her name is blessedness, and in her salutation is his salvation. But the great purpose of his life was to pay her the supreme tribute, to write of her what had never before been written of any lady, and so throughout the *Divine Comedy* he treats of her as the mirror which reflects into his soul the light of God, an illumination whereby he may find the way which leads to his true native country. The figure is plastic; God speaks at sundry times and in divers manners, and Beatrice in the *Divine Comedy* has been variously interpreted as a symbol of spiritual wisdom, of theology, the

[1] *Vide. ut sup.*, p. 93.

divine science, of the revelation of God in Scripture, of the authority of the church. She is by turns all of these, for she stands for religion in the sense of the tie which binds man to God, for union and communion with Him. As in the record of his young life, the *New Life*, so also in that of his mature experience, the *Divine Comedy*, Dante's end and object are the same, her salutation, his salvation; though his conception of the scope of these develops steadily. So it is by no new allegory, but rather by a logical continuation of the original that Beatrice, heart and reason of the pageant in the Earthly Paradise, is the symbol of the sacrament of the altar, crown and centre of all Christian worship as well as the chief means of grace and salvation; at once the burden of the church and its glory; last legacy of Christ, made possible by His twofold nature which carries earth to heaven and brings down heaven to earth.

No doubt this whole conception of the mystic procession, and especially that of the place of Beatrice in it, is disturbing, almost shocking, at first presentation. It is difficult to believe that so complex a meaning underlies the decorative details, or that Dante could have intended so to exalt Beatrice as to make her the figure of the eucharistic Christ. But modern readers have entirely lost the habit of allegory, they resent being puzzled, and so they are apt to declare not only that the color and texture of the veil are quite worth while for themselves, but to go further and say that the meaning it is said to conceal may exist only in the oversubtle mind of the inquirer. But, whatever may be the artistic value of an allegory of the Middle Ages, it is hardly fair to the men who created it to take beauty of form and color as the aim and end of their work. To them the value of it lay in the adjustment of means to end, in the vividness and accuracy with which the spiritual might be set forth through the material. At first a means of reaching the infinite through the finite, allegory came to be an obsession com-

pelling men to reverse the process and scrutinize the whole
of creation, not for its own sake but for its hidden meaning.
The most highly trained intellects of the Middle Ages
devoted themselves to this sort of interpretation and found
no created thing too humble or commonplace to illustrate
the things of the spirit. Thus finding the great mirrored in
the small, they saw themselves as close followers of their
Master who took a grain of mustard seed as the symbol of
His kingdom. Moreover, while one thing is susceptible of
half a dozen spiritual interpretations, many figures may be
required to present as many different aspects of one reality,
until at last the intricate results of this way of thinking and
writing seem to us little more than masterpieces of ingenuity.[1] But, whether we scornfully dismiss this trait as
"childish," or sentimentalize about it as "childlike," it is
always to be reckoned with in the study of medieval
literature.

This method of illustrating great truths and conveying
instruction concerning them was, of course, used in regard
to the sacraments. To Hugh of St. Victor the whole universe,
seen and unseen, from the beginning of the world to the last
judgment, was a vast and many-sided symbol of God, and
in it might be found, by him who would search humbly,
patiently, and thoroughly, the figures of that sacramental
plan of salvation, in itself a symbol of the grace and goodness
of God. Sacraments are symbolized in creation, but they

---

[1] Numerous examples of this are to be found in the *Allegoriæ in Uni-
versam sacram Scripturam* of Rabanus Maurus, *Migne*, (CXII: 849 ff).
There is no fixed connection between any one thing and its allegorical
meaning, all is fluid. For instance, butter may signify the humanity of
Christ, the teaching of the patriarchs, the contemplative life, the lust
of the flesh, the fruitfulness of a good act, the anointing with spiritual
virtues, the oil of penitence. But the humanity of Christ may be
figured by a diadem as well as by butter, while His divinity is signified
by the head, and His office as light of the world by a candlestick.
And so on indefinitely.

are at the same time symbols of hidden virtue.[1] And so Hugo leads up to the exposition of the great climax of all sacramental imagery, the eucharist.

Moreover, it was not only an age of allegory but one of dramatic interpretation as well. The mass itself is a great drama, but in the interest of even greater vividness all manner of more or less dramatic material was introduced into the celebration of it.

"From the tenth century people took all manner of liberties with the text of the Missal. It was the time of farced Kyries and Glorias, of dramatic and even theatrical ritual, of endlessly varying and lengthy prefaces, into which interminable accounts from Bible history and lives of saints were introduced. This tendency did not even spare the Canon, although the specially sacred character of this part tended to prevent people from tampering with it as recklessly as they did with other parts of the Missal."[2]

Dante is always dramatic in his presentation and he avowedly intended the use of the most complicated allegory. Moreover, he felt no irreverence whatever in identifying Beatrice as a figure of Christ, commenting on the name of her companion, Giovanna, as being the same as that of Giovanni, the Baptist, who was the forerunner of the true light of the world,[3] and putting into her mouth on the eve of her departure for Paradise the reassuring words of Christ Himself:

" *Modicum, et non videbitis me,*
Et iterum, beloved sisters mine,
Modicum, et vos videbitis me."[4]

There is surely no reason to suppose that he need have felt the slightest hesitation about taking his glorified lady

---

[1] Cf. H. O. Taylor, *The Medieval Mind,* II: 67–104.
[2] Adrian Fortescue, *Cath. Enc.,* Art. *Canon.*
[3] *Vita Nuova,* XXIV.
[4] *Purg.* XXXIII: 10–12. Also *St. John,* XVI: 16.

in the Earthly Paradise as a symbol of the sacrament in which Christ continues His presence in the church.

Nor is Dante quite alone in this conception of his lady. It has its analogies in those poems to the Virgin which in their language have so close a connection with lady worship and in which Madonna is compared to the pot of manna, to Bethlehem, the house of bread, to the ark of the covenant which contained the manna from heaven, and to the tabernacle within which was the glory of God. In several instances in the German vernacular she is addressed as the Grail, and the comparison is also carried over to the praise of the lady; the beloved one is the heart's Grail, her lover will not be alone, for she is to be to him the highest Grail which protects from every woe.[1]

X

Details of the episode tend to strengthen such an interpretation of the significance of Beatrice. She is that lady who appears veiled in white in the midst of the angelic festival.[2] In eucharistic devotion Christ is over and over again spoken of as hidden beneath the veils of bread and wine. They conceal Christ as things are concealed from us by a physical veil.[3] St. Bernard, interpreting the pillar of cloud in the wilderness, says it foretold most truly the holy sacrament in which the majesty of God, the splendor of which mortal infirmity could not bear, is veiled to our eyes.[4]

[1] For the references to these poems, but not for the inferences drawn from them, I am indebted, as I have said (p. 84), to Hertz. The text of them will be found in the Appendix, p. 134.

[2] *Purg.* XXX: 31, 65–69.

[3] "Per modum tegumenti, sicut impedimur videre id quod est velatum quocumque corporali velamine." *Summa*, Pt. III, Qu. LXXVI, Art. 7.

[4] "Quæ est autem nubes quæ præcedit vero Israelitas, nisi verissimum et sanctissimum corpus tuum quod in altari sumimus? in quo velatur nobis altitudo dei, immensitas majestatis tuæ, cujus et calorem

In the *Dialogue* of St. Catherine of Siena, Christ says to the soul: "In that place thou didst see and taste the abyss of the Trinity, whole God and whole man, concealed and veiled in that whiteness that thou sawedst in the bread." [1] The same figure is later elaborated in one of Calderon's *autos*, the *Divine Philothea*, in which the wandering prince wears a veil. This veil is lifted by Faith. When the divine Philothea mourns the departure of the prince she is assured that Faith will raise another veil so that he can still be seen by the eyes of believers. Thereupon an altar is shown with the host and chalice. This is a dramatic presentation of St. Bernard's "Glorious and beloved bride, on earth thou hast the bridegroom in the sacrament, in heaven without the veil." [2]

Seen across the stream, veiled beneath the angelic festival, Beatrice is even more beautiful than Dante's memory of her. He trembles with amazement, and it is only when the griffin's twofold image is reflected in her eyes that he can understand its meaning,[3] — that is the eucharist is the extension of the Incarnation, and only by its means can man comprehend the significance of God made man for man's salvation. This double symbolizing of Christ, as God incarnate by the griffin and as the host in Beatrice, is in harmony with the conception very often expressed in religious literature, — that Christ is both giver and gift, priest and victim.

The flowing tears, which the angels' song of hope and forgiveness brings to Dante's eyes frozen with awe of the

et splendorem mortalis infirmitas sustinere non posset, nisi mediatrix nubes interposita et ardorem desuper temperaret, et tutam subtus viam præmonstraret."— *Meditatio in passionem*, XII, *Migne*, CLXXXIV: 761.

[1] Ch. CXI, tr. Thorold.

[2] "Gloriosa et amabilis sponsa, in terra sponsum habes in sacramento, in cœlis habitura es sine velamento." — *Sermo de excellentia SS. Sacramenti, Migne*, CLXXXIV: 985.

[3] *Purg.* XXXI: 115 ff.

presence of Beatrice, have their counterpart in many lives
of the saints, for tears were regarded as a gift of grace. St.
Cuthbert, says Bede, felt compunction so deeply that he
never finished mass without a profusion of tears.[1] Thomas
Cantelupe (d. 1282) always wept profusely at mass,[2] and
Robert Winchelsy, archbishop of Canterbury, wept so in
saying mass that the corporal and altar cloth were wet.[3]
In perfect correspondence also with religious experience is
Dante's abject humility under the reproof of Beatrice which
seems to put him in jarring contrast with the crowned and
mitred lord of himself whom Virgil had brought to the
borders of the Earthly Paradise. But it is fitting that even
at the summit of human wisdom he should know the sense
of utter unworthiness which is the almost universal experience of those who approach sacramental mysteries, a feeling
which finds expression in the mass when the officiant strikes
thrice upon his breast and when he says, "Domine, non sum
dignus ut intres sub tectum meum." He also experiences
the swoon which occurs frequently among mystics, especially
when overcome with reverential awe of the sacraments.
Again, as Eve lost Paradise because she was impatient of
the veil and would fain know as God,[4] so Dante is reproved
for the steadfastness of his gaze at the veiled Beatrice;[5]
he must not seek to know more than is revealed lest he lose
the blessedness of the second Paradise — the vision of God
in its sacramental form. The subsequent commination of
the church by Beatrice has an interesting parallel in the
Dialogue of St. Catherine of Siena, in which eucharistic
enthusiasm is followed by severe condemnation of the sins
of the priesthood, doubly black in view of the fact that it
is by its agency alone that the sacramental presence of Christ
may be vouchsafed to the church. In the *Dialogue* Christ

[1] *Vita S. Cuth.* XVI. *Migne,* XCIV: 756.
[2] *Acta SS.*, Oct. 1: 603.   [4] *Purg.* XXIX: 27.
[3] Wilkins, *op. cit.* II: 489.   [5] *Ib.* XXXII: 9.

says: "Even as these ministers require cleanness in the chalice in which this Sacrifice is made, even so do I require the purity and cleanness of their heart and soul and mind." [1]

XI

All these are details, each throwing some weight on the side of eucharistic interpretation, and so worth consideration. But, after all, the most important point is the need of such an interpretation of the pageant to account for its occurrence in the *Divine Comedy* on the threshold of Paradise. So taken, it ceases to be a mere decorative intrusion, as so many readers have felt it, and assumes structural importance.

Dante, in accord with medieval theology, conceived the goal of man to be the blessedness of eternal life, and this consists in the fruition of the divine aspect, the vision of God in the celestial Paradise. There man like the angels will see God face to face. In this world he must be content to see as in a glass darkly, he needs means adapted to his present limitations. The whole mount of Purgatory as Dante climbs it shows the service of the church in providing such means. He hears at every terrace the prayers and hymns of the liturgy, passes through the sacrament of penance as a gate, and is constantly reminded of the Christian classification of sins and virtues. Using the means of grace thus offered, he passes into the Earthly Paradise, the goal of the ascent of Purgatory even as the Empyrean is the goal of the ascent through the spheres. This Earthly Paradise signifies to him the blessedness of this life, and the fathers very generally considered it to represent the church. The blessedness of the heavenly Paradise is the full vision of God. In what vision is the blessedness of the Earthly Paradise, the church?

[1] Ch. CXI, tr. Thorold. Cf. the discussion on sacerdotal purity, p. 69.

What, indeed, but the vision in the eucharist, the supreme means by which the faithful, purified in heart, may see God even in this life?[1] This view appears in a passage from Hugh of St. Victor, great scholastic mystic, honored by Dante in *Paradise*.[2] He says there are three paradises: the first is that of man's innocence, and in it was the material tree of life; the second is the church, and of it the tree of life is Christ Who gave His life on the cross and gives it daily in the eucharist; the third is the paradise of God, whereof the tree is the divine wisdom, fountain of life and origin of all good;[3] in other words, knowledge of God, life eternal.

That the allegorical presentation of the sacramental *visio Dei* should centre in Beatrice is as logical as inevitable.[4] Dante was churchman and theologian, finding his salvation in the means of grace provided in the church; but he was

---

[1] Cf. the vision attributed to Thomas Aquinas by Lydgate in *A Procession of Corpus Christi:*

> "Þis hoolly Thomas, called of Algwyne,
> By hie myracle þat sawghe persones three,
> An ooste ful rounde, a sunne about it shyne,
> Joyned in oon by parfyte vnytee,
> A gloryous likenesse of þe Trynitee,
> Gracyous and digne for to beo comended,
>   With feyth, with hope, with parfyte charitee,
> Al oure byleeve is þere Inne comprehended."

Minor Poems of Lydgate, ed. McCracken, p. 42. Cf. also frontispiece in which the centre shows the rose crown of Paradise enclosing the Trinity. Above are three visions of God on earth — St. Francis receiving the *stigmata*; the holy face of St. Veronica and the mass of St. Gregory — a transubstantiation miracle. *Vide* pp. 78, 79.

[2] *Par.* XII: 133.

[3] *De Arca Noe Morali*, III: XVII., *Migne*, CLXXVI: 646. For text *vide*. App. p. 136.

[4] The conception of Dante's love for Beatrice as a religious experience is developed by Professor J. B. Fletcher, *Religion of Beauty in Women*, pp. 30 ff. I have done little more than work out this experience in terms of sacramental devotion.

no less of the school of the *dolce stil nuovo*, which adding to
the lady worship of Provence a spiritual quality, found in
the beauty of the beloved a path leading to the essence of
beauty, goodness reflecting God. At his first glimpse of her
he knew that his beatification had come to him.[1] She is
called Beatrice by many who knew not wherefore. Her
salutation is to him salvation, and its withdrawal leaves
him utterly desolate, excommunicate. Only when he has
learned to ask nothing for himself and to devote himself to
her praise can he find the way to true union:

"Ladies, the end and aim of my Love was but the salutation of
that lady of whom I conceive that ye are speaking; wherein alone
I found that beatitude which is the goal of desire. And now that it
hath pleased her to deny me this, Love, my Master, of his great
goodness, hath placed all my beatitude where my hope will not fail
me." [2]

Losing his young life and love he kept it "unto life eternal." In the *New Life* he had found the love of God in
loving her; in the *Divine Comedy* he comes to the knowledge
of God through knowing her. He had hoped to write concerning his lady what had not before been written of any
woman; and so, when he came to celebrate the praise of
the eucharist — glory of the Earthly Paradise, the church
— the sacrament which is the foretaste of the beatific vision,
he could personify it under no other form than that of the
lady who had led him to blessedness in his youth and by
whose hand he hoped still to be led to gaze continually on
His countenance "Qui est per omnia sæcula benedictus."

[1] *Vita Nuova*, I.

[2] Tr. Rossetti. "Madonne, lo fine del mio amore fu già il saluto di
questa donna, forse di cui voi intendete, ed in quello dimorava la beatitudine, ch'è il fine di tutti li miei desiri. Ma poi che le piacque di
negarlo a me, lo mio signore, Amore, la sua mercede, ha posta tutta la
mia beatitudine in quello, che non mi puote venir meno." — *Vita Nuova*,
XVIII.

XII

To recapitulate briefly this special study of the closing cantos of the *Purgatory:* we have a scene set in the Earthly Paradise, to reach which Dante has climbed the weary heights of purification. In it he sees a great pageant, strikingly like those processions of the blessed sacrament of which the greatest is that of Corpus Christi day. The chariot of the church, drawn by Christ, serves to bring into the picture the veiled figure of Beatrice, who occupies the central position accorded the host in such processions and who is hailed in the very words used daily in the mass to greet the coming of Christ to the altar at the moment of consecration. If Beatrice is here what these words imply, namely the symbol of transubstantiation, by which God continues to dwell with men, which affords the highest degree of illumination possible to the human soul this side of the beatific vision, then indeed is the Earthly Paradise type and pledge of the heavenly. The glory of both is the same; in the one, as runs the language of the mass, the "Lamb of God who taketh away the sins of the world;" in the other, as the *Apocalypse* declares,[1] "the Lamb is the light thereof." The reward of both is the vision of God; here below in the sacramental mirror, in the glass darkly; there, face to face. The eucharistic vision must share the imperfection of all our vision here, but it is still the foretaste and earnest of that *visio Dei* to be fulfilled in Paradise, the complete illumination of the soul, salvation, beatitude, the goal of man.

> " Qui nobis das tam dulcia
> prægustando præludia,
> te frui des in patria
> beata nobis gaudia." [2]

[1] *Rev.* xxi: 23.   [2] Hymn, *Jesu, nostra refectio*, Daniel, IV; 271.

APPENDICES

APPENDICES

I. THE EUCHARIST AS A MEANS TO
THE VISION OF GOD [1]

Dionysius calls the second part of his work the *ecclesiastical* rather than the *earthly* hierarchy, because the second has the same heavenly scope and end as the first, — the union with God. But as man is incapable of the direct knowledge of God vouchsafed to the heavenly orders he is mercifully provided with symbols whereby he may be brought to such degree of knowledge as is possible for him. To these symbols he is led by the divinely appointed ecclesiastical hierarchy, the custodian of them.

Like the *Celestial Hierarchy* the *Ecclesiastical* is composed of Triads.

I. The three great symbolic sacraments: (*a*) Baptism, which is purification; (*b*) The Eucharist (synaxis) which is illumination; (*c*) Unction, which is perfecting.

II. Bishops, Priests, Deacons.

III. (*a*) Illuminated monks, who are perfected. (*b*) Initiated laymen, who are illuminated. (*c*) Catecumens, who are purified.

He works out the first two sacraments very carefully, but does very little with the third. The process by which the neophyte is taken by the ecclesiastical authority and led to the waters of purification is elaborated with a symbolic interpretation of every step in the liturgy, and the eucharist is treated in the same way.

The first passage mentioned in the text treats of the sacraments as the mirrors by means of which God is revealed to man, and runs as follows:

Cæterum sublimiores istæ naturæ ordinesque, quarum venerandam supra feci mentionem, et incorporeæ sunt, et spiritalis ac supermundialis sacer illarum magistratus existit; nostrum vero

[1] *Vide* p. 20.

cernimus, diversa ab ipsis ratione, sensibilium varietate signorum multiplicari, quibus sacrosancte ad uniformem deiformitatem pro captu nostro, et ad Deum divinamque virtutem promovemur. Istæ quidem, utpote mentes, prout illis fas est intelligunt; nos vero a sensu perceptis imaginibus ad divinas, quantum possumus, contemplationes sublevamur. Et ut vere dicam, unum quidem est, quod omnes qui deiformes sunt appetunt, ejus tamen, quod omnino unum atque idem est, non unimode participes existunt, sed prout cuilibet pro merito sortem divina trutina distribuit. I: ii.

Ecclesiastical Hierarchy, Migne P. G. 111: 370 ff.

The next closes with a prayer for true knowledge of the eucharist:

Cæterum his, quæ aditorum vestibulis eleganter adpicta rudiorum contemplationi satis sunt, relictis, ab effectis ad causas progrediemur, deinde sacram nostram synaxin, atque consentaneam rerum spiritalium, Jesu prælucente, contemplationem conspicabimur, beatam primitivorum pulchritudinem præclare prorsus evibrantem. Sed tu, o divinissimum ac sacrosanctum sacramentum, circumposita tibi, symbolice ænigmatum operimenta revelans, liquido nobis manifesteris, mentalesque nostros obtutus singulari et aperta luce adimpleto. III: ii.

And the last connects sacramental union with the fruition of God:

Est autem hæc deificatio, Dei quædam, quoad fieri potest, assimilatio unioque. Omni porro ordini sacro communis scopus est, erga Deum et res divinas continua delectio, quæ divinitus seritur, et per ejus unionem consummatur, quæque hac prior est, illi adversantium omnimoda et irrevertibilis fuga, cognitio rerum qua res sunt, sacræ veritatis visio scientiaque, simplicis perfectionis ejus qui summe simplex est, divina participatio, fruitio intuitionis, quæ omnem sui contemplatorem spiritali modo reficit deificatque. I: iii.

II. THE "RITUAL" THEORY [1]

The theories advanced by Dr. Nitze[2] and Miss Weston[3] are important contributions to recent Grail criticism, and seem at first sight to present a radically new departure. Both critics believe the Grail legends are based on agrarian cults, but Professor Nitze holds that the clew to the origin of the story is to be found in the Eleusinian mysteries, and Miss Weston thus expresses herself: "While admitting the value of much of Dr. Nitze's work, and the light it has thrown on certain features of the legend, I cannot admit that the Eleusinian cult provides us with as satisfactory an explanation of the peculiar features and incidents of the Grail story as may be found in the more widely diffused Adonis ritual." [4]

All workers in the Grail material may well be grateful for the light the research connected with these theories has thrown on it. It is particularly helpful that so many apparently irrelevant details in the narratives are explained by it. But one may willingly grant that there are many elements of fertility rites preserved in the Grail story and still believe that these elements came into it through the medium of Christian worship, and that the storytellers were absolutely without consciousness as to their origin. I had done some work on this hypothesis before becoming aware of that of Miss Peebles.[5] She has carefully considered many of the points in which I am interested, especially the analogies between the Grail ritual and the early liturgies of the Christian church. I should, however, like to call attention to additional material which seems to me to strengthen her arguments and may, perhaps, bring in elements untouched by her.

It should be noted, in the first place, that many modern historians of the eucharist not only admit its connection with earlier rites, but even rejoice that the Christian sacrament was at once the beginning of a new dispensation and the fulfilment, not only of the law and the prophets of the Old Testament, but also of the

---

[1] *Vide* p. 39.
[2] *Proceedings of the Modern Language Association*, XXIV.
[3] *Legend of Sir Perceval* and the *Quest of the H. G.*
[4] *Quest of the H. G.*, pp. 131 f.
[5] *Legend of Longinus*, pp. 195–221.

world-wide ceremonies which expressed the aspiration of primitive man to share in the perpetual miracle of life.[1]

Coming from primitive sacrifice to the more organized rites of the Eleusinian mysteries we find them also recognized as forerunners of Christian rites and ceremonies:

"The influence of the mysteries, and of the religious cults which were analogous to the mysteries, was not simply general; they modified in some important respects the Christian sacraments of baptism and the eucharist."[2]

"It seems fair to infer that, since there were great changes in the ritual of the sacraments, and since the new elements of these changes were identical with elements that already existed in cognate and largely diffused forms of worship, the one should be due to the other."[3]

Religious ceremony inherited from the remote past of the race has, as a rule, a double history. The symbolism by which man

---

[1] "When the eucharist was instituted the idea of communion with God by means of a sacred meal had long been familiar. Among the Greeks this idea underlay the mystic food and drink in the mysteries of Eleusis. All over the world this has furnished the highest point of savage rites." — Darwell Stone, *History of the Doctrine of the Holy Eucharist*, I: 2.

The question is also considered by a conservative contemporary writer, Bishop Brent: "In order that we may arrive at the simple meaning which contains all other meanings, let us consider the origin of sacrificial feasts of which the Holy Communion is the final development. We shall not think solely of what can be learned from a study of Jewish sacrifices, but shall include what has been revealed by a study of comparative religions." After discussing the religious use of meat as food he says: "Jesus Christ gathers up the primitive thoughts of our savage untutored ancestors and explains them. He lays hold of their gropings in the dark and illumines them." — *The Revelation of Discovery*, pp. 100–102. *Vide* also H. C. Trumbull, *The Blood Covenant*, especially pp. 271–293; A. C. L. Brown, *From Cauldron of Plenty to Grail, Modern Philology*, XIV: 7.

[2] Hatch, *The Influence of Greek Ideas and Usages upon the Christian Church*, p. 294. Cf. also A. E. J. Rawlinson, in *Foundations*, pp. 181–198.

[3] *Ib.*, p. 305.

has once expressed either his experience or his aspirations is never lost, but in varying forms and modifications still answers his need. But while on the one hand it amounts with him to the highest flights of worship, on the other it descends into the pit from which it was digged and becomes the magic rite, the charm, the *taboo*. The ritual of the eucharist is no exception to this. From the barest Lord's Supper to the Pontifical High Mass it is the great ceremonial expression of man's aspiration to God. At the same time it has been reduced to the service of sheer superstition.[1]

That features derived from primitive worship were conspicuous in the eucharistic rites of the early British church is more than probable.[2] That the Celtic story of the quest for a vessel of increase, very likely itself a feature of early agrarian rites, was colored by the rites of a more or less corrupted Christianity may very well be true. Moreover, there is no doubt whatever, as has just been said, of the value of the study of these primitive rites in accounting for many apparently irrelevant details of the narrative. But such admissions by no means allow the claim that there was a conscious survival of fertility rites of which the Grail legend is a record; that de Borron was an "initiate" of such rites, treating his subject from the "inside," as Miss Weston maintains;[3] nor that knowledge of any such illicit ritual accounts for the admitted coldness of the ecclesiastical authorities to the legend.

[1] For example, the custom in some parts of Germany where the priest, with the host suspended from his neck in a bag, rode around the fields on Whitsunday praying for the fertility of the fields. This finds a literary expression:

"In villages the husbandmen about their corne doe ride,
   With many Crosses, Banners, and Sir John their Priest beside;
   — Who in a bag about his necke doth beare the blessed breade."

Fourth Booke of the Popish Kingdom or reigne of Antichrist written in Latine verse by Thomas Naogeorgus (or Kirschmeier) and englyshed by Barnabe Googe, Anno 1570. Cæsarius of Heisterbach (*op. cit.* IX: ix,) gives instances of the use of the host as a charm. He tells of a woman who, desiring to improve her garden, abstracted a host at the time of communion and buried it among the cabbages.

[2] *Vid. ut. sup.*, p. 51. Cf. also Miss Peebles, *op. cit.*, pp. 203–216.

[3] *Legend of Sir Perceval*, II: 279.

As to this last point it may be said that it is not at all surprising that Norman ecclesiastics were not enthusiastic about the Grail story. They were heart and soul in favor of Roman supremacy and not likely to approve of the audacious claim that Joseph of Arimathea brought to Britain special instructions as to the eucharist. Nor would they at all care for the implication that the special usage of the Celtic church, which they steadily strove to extirpate with such success that we cannot be at all sure of its exact nature, had any such divine authorization. Neither politically nor religiously could they welcome a narrative embodying any such claims.

I have already said something as to Miss Weston's points concerning the celibacy of Alain[1] and the "secret" of the Grail.[2] I should like, in conclusion, to add a rejoinder to her assertion that "no Catholic writer of the twelfth or twentieth century would dare to transport the 'Mystery of the Mass' to a banqueting hall and make it the centre of a roman d'aventure: there are things *qui ne se font pas*, and this is one of them."[3]

It is well known that the church has always been obliged to restrict very carefully the privilege of celebrating mass in private chapels as well as that of having the host reserved in great houses. The use of portable altars was limited because of abuse in this very direction. Giraldus Cambrensis is so very explicit as to where mass may be said as to make it evident that usage in this respect was very loose in the Welsh marches.[4] But there is incidental evidence that, from the romancer's point of view, there was nothing surprising or shocking in the idea of having the reserved host in close proximity to, if not actually within the banqueting hall. In *Perlesvaus* (XXXV: iv), the hermits march into the royal hall in white garments with a red cross on the breast. As soon as they enter "il annorèrent Deu nostre Seingnor et batirent lor coupes." They beat their breasts, "mea culpa, mea maxima culpa," the gesture of utter humility and unworthiness before the host, made also by Arthur when he was privileged to see the child on the altar at mass (*ib.*, I: vi), and "commança Dieu à proier et à battre sa coupe." It was God our Lord in the host Who was thus honored,

[1] *Ut sup.*, p. 74.
[2] *Ut sup.*, p. 65.
[3] *Op cit.*, p. 300 n.
[4] *Gemma Eccl.*, I: vii.

but the romancer evidently had no feeling of irreverence in introducing this custom into his narrative; nor is there good reason to suppose there would have been any more hesitation in utilizing for literary purposes a more elaborate ceremonial centring in eucharistic devotion.

III. THE RELICS OF JOSEPH OF ARIMATHEA REMOVED FROM MOIENMOUTIERS[1]

Tempore Karoli Magni, vir quidam venerabilis, Fortunatus nomine, patriarcha Hierosolymitanus, corpus S. Josephi decurionis, sepultoris domini, paganos qui tunc terram sanctam vastabunt fugiens, apportavit et ad Medianum monasterium deveniens, ibidem cum ipsis reliquiis se collocavit. Sed postmodum, ipsum sancti corpus, per insolentiam canonicorum qui illum locum possiderunt, a quibusdam monachis peregrinis noctu furatum, asportatum est. Et ita illud monasterium tali est thesauro viduatum.

Richer, *Senon. mon. chronicon.* II: 6; *cit.*, P. Paris, *Romania*, I: 457.

IV. THE DISCOVERY OF ARTHUR'S TOMB AT GLASTONBURY[2]

Ad ann. 1193, de corpore Arthuri magni dicitur quod circa hunc annum sit inventum in Anglia in insula Avalonis ubi est Abbatia sancti Dunstani Glastonia vulgariter dicta ad sanctum Petrum de Glastemberin, Batoniensis diocesis, et hoc factum est per industriam cujusdam monachi ejusdem ecclesiæ novi Abbatis qui totum cimiterium loci diligenter excavando fecit investigari, animatus verbis, quæ olim (adhuc) monachus audiverat ab ore Henrici patris Richardi, et inventa est tumba lapidea in profundo terræ defossa, super quam lamina plumbea quibusdam versibus erat insignata

> Hic jacet Arturus, flos Regum gloria Regni,
> Quem probitas morum commendat laude perenni;
> Hic jacet Arturus Britonum rex ultor inultus.

Alberic des Trois Fontaines, *cit.* San Marte, *Essuy*, p. 17.

[1] *Vide* p. 49. [2] *Vide* p. 49.

V. THE EARLIEST KNOWN USE OF THE WORD "TRANSUBSTANTIATION"[1]

The text is Hosea XII: 10. *In manibus prophetarum assimilatus sum.* The following passage occurs towards the end: "Cum intro ad altare Dei, spectaculum factus sum Deo, et angelis, et hominibus; si pollutus sto carne et spiritu, quam abominabilis sum! Attendamus. Antiochus Epiphanes idolum posuit in templo Domini, obquam abominationem non licuit sacrificare in templo donec initiatum fuerit. In hunc modum, si fuero vas incontinentiæ et libidinis, in altari juxta filium Virginis statuo filium Veneris. Cum profero verba Canonis, et verbum transubstationis, et os meum plenum est contradictione, et amaritudine, et dolo, quamvis eum honorem labiis, tamen spuo in faciem Salvatoris. Cum præsumo sumere Dominum meum, et panem in os meum sic pollutum, levius est in projicerem eum in lutum platearum. Itaque mundamini, qui fertis vasa Domini; mundamini qui refertis verba Domini; qui offertis hostiam Domini; mundamini, qui defertis aliis corpus Domini, ut mundati quod nunc similitudine geritis, quandoque rerum veritate capiatis.

Hildebert of Lavardin, *Sermones de diversis*, VI.
Migne, CLXXI: 772.

VI. ARTHUR SEES A CHILD ON THE ALTAR AT MASS[2]

At ubi incepit dictus senex Missam, et venit usque ad offertorium, statim benigna Domina filium sacerdoti obtulit. Sacerdos vero eum collocavit super corporale, juxta calicem. Cum autem prevenisset ad immolationem hostiæ, id est, ad verba Dominica, *Hoc est enim corpus meum*, elevavit eundem puerum in manibus suis. Rex vero Arthurus stans ad sacramentum illud Dominicum, immo vere ipsum Dominum, suppliciter adorabat.

Johannis Glastoniensis, *Chronica sive Historia de Rebus Glastoniensibus*, ed. Tho. Hearnius. Oxonii, 1716. 1: 79.

[1] *Vide* p. 70.   [2] *Vide* p. 77.

VI. THE CHRIST OF ST. GREGORY[1]

Il uit celui homme crucefije en la crois que li angeles tenoit et les cleus quil auoit ueu tenir al autre angele li estoient es pies et es mains et la che[i]nture quil auoit entor lui si sambloit bien a icele eure home qui fust en angoisse de mort. Apres regarda ioseph[e] que la lance quil auoit ueue tenir al tiers angele estoit fichie parmi le cors al homme crucefie si en degoutoit contreual la hanste vns ruissiaus qui nestoit ne tout sanc ne tout aigue ne porquant si sambloit ce a estre sanc et aigue. Et desous ses pies au crucefijet iut icele escuele que ioseph ses peires auoit eportee en larche si li estoit auis que li sans des pies al crucefije degoutoit en cele escuele.

Grand St. Graal, ed. Sommer, pp. 32, 33.

Lors regardent li compaignon et vo[i]ent issir del vaissel .j. home qui auoit les mains sanglentes et les pies et le cors si lor dist. Mi cheualier et mi seriant et mi fil loial qui en ceste mortel vie estes deuenu esperitel vous maues tant quis que iou ne me puis plus vers vous celer si conuient que vous vees partie de mes repostailles et de mes secres.

Queste, ed. Sommer, p. 190.

Atant ez-vous les deus damoiseles qui reviennent devent la table et senble à monseignor Gauvain qu'il an avoit III et esgarde contremont et li sanble estre li Graaus touz an char, et voit par deseure, ce li est avis, un roi couronné, clofichié an une croiz, et li estoit li glaives fichiez el costé.

Perlesvaus, VI: xx

VIII. THE MYSTIC VISION IN THE GRAIL[2]

Li preudons . . . commencha la messe. Et quant il ot faite sa beneichon si prent corpus domini et fait signe a bohort quil viegne auant. Et il si fait sagenoille deuant lui. Et quant il i est venus li preudons li dist . bohort vois tu ce que ie tieng . Sire fait il oi bien. Je voi que vous tenes mon salueor et ma redemption en samblance

[1] *Vide* p. 79.   [2] *Vide* p. 82.

de pain. Et en tel maniere nel viesse ie mie. Mais mi oeil sont si terrien quil ne peuent veoir les espirituels choses (ne il) nel me laissent (autrement) veoir ains me tolent la vraie samblance. Car de ce ne dout ie mie (que ce ne soit) vraie chars et vrais homs et enterriene deites. lors commencha a plorer trop durement.

Queste, ed. Sommer, pp. 119, 120.

Et quant il ot este grant piece a ienols si se leua et commencha la messe de la glorieuse meire dieu . et quant il vint el secre de la mes(s)e . et il ot ostee la platine de desus le saint veissel si apela galaad et li dist . vien auant serians ihesu crist . si verras ce que tu as tant desire a veoir. Et il se traist auant et regarde deuant (dedens) le saint vaissel et si tost comme il ot . j. foi regarde si commencha a trambler moult durement si tost comme la mortels char commencha a regarder les esperitels choses. Lors tent galaad ses mains vers le ciel si dist . Sire toi crie iou merci quant tu mas acompli mon voloir. Car or voi iou tout apertement ce que langue ne poroit dire ne cuers penser. Ici voi iou locoison de proeces et les merueilles de toutes les autres . et puis quil est ensi bials dous sires que vos maues acompli mes voloirs de veoir ce que iai tos iors desire.

Ib., p. 197.

IX. DATE OF THE CORPUS CHRISTI PROCESSION ACCORDING TO CATALANI[1]

viii. De eo tandem quod Grancolas scribit, delatam in Gallia primum post annum MCCC Eucharistiam in solemni processione fuisse, videri potest eruditissimus Lupus, Tomo XI, Operum editionis Venetæ in Dissertatione *De sacris Processionibus*, Cap. III, ubi fuse ostendit Urbanum IV. Processionem licet non præceperat, omnino tamen probasse, ac in Italia inchoasse.

ix. Sed ut hanc rem uberius nos prosequamur, tametsi nonnulli addubitent, an ab Urbano simul cum ipso Festo sanctissimi Sacramenti instituta fuerit processio, quia scilicet de illa ab Urbano in sua Constitutione nulla fiat mentio, probabilius est, quod Clarissimi Auctores docent, utrique solemnitatis auctorem fuisse, quippe cum publica processio ex communi Ecclesiæ usu ad Festi solemnitatem

[1] *Vide* p. 95.

pertineat, ut docet Jacobus Eveillon in Libro, *De processionibus Ecclesiasticis*, Capite XVIII. Urbano quidem in ipsa institutione ea mens fuit, ut omni genere solemnitatis, et plene, ut loquitur, hoc festum celebraretur. Et certe plausus ille populorum, et publica omnium ordinum tripudatio, exultatio, et jubilatio, quæ in celebratione hujus festi commemorantur a laudato Pontifice, non æque videntur posse convenire divinis Officiis, quæ statarie, ut ajunt, in Choro a solis Clericis canuntur, ac pompæ ipsi processionis; et in sola evectione Sanctissimi Sacramenti, quæ fit procedendo per vias, et loca publica, cernitur imago triumphi illius Christi, cujus causa ipsemet Institutor Urbanus, et Tridentini Concilii Patres Sessione XIII Cap. v. dicunt institutum fuisse hoc festum ad confundendam specialiter hæreticorum perfidiam, atque insaniam.

x. Sunt quidem in hac sententia, non modo memoratus Lupus, et Jacobus Eveillon in laudato Libro, Cap. XXV. verum etiam Joannes Luziardus in *Epitome Historiæ universalis*, Cap. CCXXXIII, Hermanus Scheder in *Chronicis* in VI ætate mundi, Philippus Bergomas in supplemento *Chronicorum*, Onuphrius Panvinius in Additionibus ad Platinam in *Vita Urbani* IV, Fredericus Nausea in *Catechismo Catholico Lib.* VI, Capit XXXVIII. Joannes Molanus in *Natalibus Sanctorum Belgii* die v Aprilis, Alphonsus Ciaconius in *Vitis Pontificum*, ubi agit de Urbano IV. Henricus Spondanus in continuatione *Annalium Cardinalis Baronii* anno Christi MCCLXIV et alii, qui docent, Urbanum IV Romanum Pontificem Maximum instituisse solemnitatem Corporis Christi cum Processionibus, et Octavis a cunctis fidelibus celebrari.

Catalani, *Pontificale Romanum*, Vol. II: 311.

X. EUCHARISTIC PROCESSIONS [1]

(a) *Palm Sunday*

Cantata tertia legatur Evangelium *Turba multa*. Postea accedens abbas, aut sacerdos, benedicat palmas, et flores et frondes ante majus altare supra tapetum posita, acqua benedicta aspergat, et incenset. Accedentes secretarii distribuant ea, palmas abbati, et prioribus, et personis honestioribus, flores et frondes cæteris.

[1] *Vide* p. 96.

Interim cantore incipiente, cantatur antiphona *Pueri Hebræorum* et alia, *Pueri Hebræorum.* His ita expletis profiscatur processio, cantore incipiente quæ ad hanc processionem cantari oportet. Qua de choro exeunte, pulsentur omnia signa. Præcedant famuli cum vexillis, sequatur conversus (j. novitius), ferens situlam cum acqua benedicta, alii duo portantes duas cruces; item duo cum duobus candelabris accensis desuper cereis, alii duo ferentes duo thuribula igne et thure referta. . . . Ipse enim distribuit quæ portanda sunt, et processionem ordinat. Hos sequantur duo subdiaconi portantes duos textus Evangeliorum. Post quos laici monachi, deinde infantes cum magistris. Post quos cæteri fratres præcedentes abbatem qui ultimos procedit, duo et duo, sicut sunt priores.

Hæc sunt quæ ad hanc processionem cantanda sunt, vel omnia, vel quantum permiserit spatium loci quo ituri sunt; *Ante sex dies: Cum appropinquaret, Prima autem azymorum, Dominus Jesus, Cogitaverunt, Cum audisset populus, omnes collaudent.* Cum autem preventum fuerit ad ipsum locum, fiat statio a toto conventu. Cantore autem incipiente antiphonam *Occurrunt turbæ,* exeant duo sacerdotes albis induti, qui portent feretrum, quod parum ante diem ab eisdem sacerdotibus illuc debet esse delatum, in quo et corpus Christi esse debet reconditum. Ad quod feretrum præcedant statim qui vexilla portant et cruces et cætera quæ superius dicta sunt. Et stantibus iis qui feretrum portant, stabunt et ipsi a dextra et a sinistra ipsius feretri, ordinate sicut venerunt. Pueri vero accedentes stabunt, versis vultibus ad ipso reliquos, cum magistris suis et quibusdam cantoribus qui auxilio eis esse possunt. Majores vero versi erunt ad invicem, eo modo quo in choro stare solent. Sic autem ordinetur hæc statio, ut modicum intervallium sit inter pueros et majorem conventum. Finita antiphona *occurrunt turbæ,* incipiant pueri et qui cum eis sunt antiphonam *Hosanna filio David* flectentes genua et in principio, et in fine antiphonæ, quia in utroque *Hosanna* dicitur. Quam antiphonam chorus repetat, et similiter genua flectat. Deinde a pueris cantetur antiphona *cum angelis,* in fine tantum antiphonæ genua flectentibus. Quæ antiphona a conventu repetatur et similiter venia accipiatur.

Taliter his peractis, abbate vel cantore incipiente antiphonam

Ave, rex noster, transeant portitores feretri per medium stationis, præcedentibus his qui vexilla portant, et cæteris superius dictis portitoribus, servato ab omnibus ordine in redeundo quem habuerunt in eundo. Quibus transeuntibus flectent genua, non simul omnes, sed singuli hinc et inde, sicut feretrum transibit ante eos. Percantata hac antiphona, cantent et alia, si spatium loci plura poposcerit. Cum venerint ad portas civitatis stationem faciant, separatis ab invicem, prout locus patietur, utrisque lateribus, feretrum vero ante introitum portarum sic ponatur super mensam pallio coopertam ut prædicti portitores, ex utroque latere stantes, habeant ad feretrum in medio eorum positum versas facies suas. Locus vero super introitum portarum honeste debet este paratus, et cortinis (aulæis *seu* tapetibus) et dorsalibus.

Taliter ordinata statione, canant pueri de loco apto, et qui præcepto cantoris cum eis erunt *Gloria laus*, et similiter chorus respondeat. *Pueri, Israel es tu Rex* et chorus, *Cui puerile decus;* item pueri, *Plebs Hebræa tibi*, et chorus, Cui *puerile*, item pueri, Cœtus *in excelsis*, et chorus *Gloria laus*. His dictis inchoet cantor responsorium *Ingrediente Domine;* et, ingrediente civitatem processione, duo majora signa pulsentur, donec cætera signa, processione intrante in chorum, pulsentur ad missam. Sic ordinata processio, veniens usque ante portas monasterii, faciat stationem, servantibus pueris ordinem suum inter utrumque chorum. Deponatur iterum feretrum super mensam pallio coopertam. Cantor vero sic antea incœptum habeat responsorium *Collegerunt pontificies* ut tunc prope cantum sit; quo cantato tres aut quattuor fratres, induti cappis quas secretarius ibi paratas habeat, canant versum *Unus autem ex ipsis*, stantes inter chorum et reliquias. Quo finito, cum regressu intrent ecclesiam, cantore inchoante antiphonam *Principeo*, et aliam *Appropinquabat*. Et ingressi Ecclesiam faciant stationem per omnia similem ante Crucifixum prius detectum. Atque ibi a tribus vel quatuor fratribus cantetur in cappis responsorium *Circumdederunt*. Quo cantato incipiat abbas responsorium *Synagogæ*, et intrent chorum sonantibus ad missam signis, missam celebrent, palmas et frondes in manibus habeant, easque post oblationem panis et vini, incipiente diacono, cuncti per ordinem offerant.

Lanfranc, *Decreti pro ordine S. Benedicti, Migne*, CL, 455 ff.

(*b*) *In Connection with the Easter Sepulchre*

Processio cum eucharistia ante, vel post nocturnas Paschalis vigilias.

viii. Ab hoc ritu haud multum absimilis est processio SS. Sacramenti quam ita descriptam exhibet Ordinarium insignis Ecclesiæ Laudunensis: (In die Paschæ ad matutinum duæ magnæ campanæ de miraculis insimul pulsantur. Processio vadit ad sepulchrum ordinata in modum qui sequitur. Primo præcedit clericulus aquam benedictam deferens, hunc sequuntur duo clericuli ferentes cereos: duo alii clericuli cappis sericis induti ferentes duas cruces aureas, hos sequuntur clericuli. Deinde cantor et succentor cappis sericis induti, portantes baculos deargentatos in manibus. Deinde duo diaconi similiter cappis sericis induti, pallium supra brachium tenentes. Hos sequuntur alii combinati: unusquisque cereum accensum deferens. Prædicti vero diaconi ad ostium sepulcri venientes incipiunt *ardens est.* Clericulus stans in sepulcro respondet *Qvem quæritis?* Diaconi *Jesum Nazárenum.* Clericulus *Non est hic.* Postea cantor et succentor incipiunt *Surrexit Dominus vere alleluja.* Deinde psal. *Victimæ Paschali laudes.* Et sic cantando procedunt ante crucifixum in medio Ecclesiæ, sacerdos alba casula vestitus, portans calicem cum Corpore Christi, egrediens de sepulcro reperit ante ostium quatuor subdiaconos, albis tunicis indutos, pallium super baculum tollentes, et illo protectus incedit in fine processionis, præcedentibus duobus clericulis cum cereis, et aliis duobus juxta ipsum cum thuribulis. Dum autem processio pervenerit in medio Ecclesiæ, cantor et succentor incipiunt ℟ *Christus resurgens.* Duo diaconi cantant v *Dicant nunc.* Quo cantato, processio intrat chorum cantando *Quod enim vivit.* Sacerdos calicem super altare deponit. Interim campanæ simul pulsantur, Episcopus stans in cathedra mitra et cappa præparatus incipit *Domine labia mea aperies.*)

ix. Hic ritus Corporis Christi cum solemni pompa hac die in processione deferendi non uni fuit Laudunentis Ecclesiæ singularis, sed multis etiam aliis communis, ut Suessionensi et Remensi, apud quam tam in cathedrali B. Mariæ, quam in monachorum S. Remigii basilica adhuc hodie viget. Viget etiam nunc in Ecclesia Aurelianensi et apud Armoricos in Rotonensi monasterio. Illius praxim videre est in *Vita S. Udalrici Augustensis Episcopi*, in cujus capite 4, hæc lego: (Desiderantissimo atque sanctissimo Paschali die adveniente, post Primam intravit Ecclesiam S. Ambrosi, ubi die Parasceve Corpus Christi superposito, lapide collocavit, ibique cum paucis clericis missam de Sancta Trinitate explevit. Expleta autem missa, clerum interim congregatum, in scena juxta eamdem Ecclesiam sitam solemnissimis vestibus indutum antecisset, secum portato Corpore Christi, et evangelio, et cereis, et incenso, et cum congrua salutatione versum a pueris decantata, per atrium perrexit ad Ecclesiam S. Joannis Baptistæ.) In pervetusto etiam libro rituali Parthenonsis Pictaviensis S. Crucis hæc reperio: (In prima vigilia noctis Paschæ duo presbyteri revestiti cum cappis pergunt ad sepulchrum. . . . Inde elevatur et defertur Corpus Dominicum ad majus altare, præcedentibus cereis et thuribulis, et pulsantibus signis.)

Martène, Ec. Rit., Lib. IV; Cap. XXV.

XI. THE INTROIT AND ITS RITUAL SIGNIFICANCE [1]

At high (or sung) mass till quite lately the rule had obtained that the choir did not begin the Introit till the celebrant began the first prayers at the foot of the altar. Now the new Vatican "Gradual" (1908) has restored the old principle, that it is to be sung while the procession moves from the sacristy to the altar.

A. Fortescue, Cath. Enc., Art. Introit.

De introitu et processione ministrorum

Sacerdote ad altare ingressuro debet tota præsens Ecclesia dilatare animam suam, et amplioris fidei sinu memoriam incarnationis tenere, et sanctorum qui eum ab initio mundi exspectaverunt, et ejus adventum suspiriis, laudibus atque precibus expetierunt memor esse, et eorum contemplatione in voces erumpere præcinendo Antiphonam quæ dicitur *Ad introitum.* Nam sicut Introitus sacerdotis, ingressum Filii Dei in mundum hunc, sic

[1] *Vide* p. 102.

Antiphona quæ dicitur *Ad introitum,* voces et exspectationem præfert patriarcharum et prophetarum. In Processione quæ significatæ rei aptissime congruit, præcedunt flammantes cerei, in signum et memoriam quod per adventum Christi *sedentibus in regione umbræ mortis lux orta est eis.* (*Isa.* II.) Præveniunt sacerdotes ministri duo, non pariter neque a latere incessum coæquantes, sed ante subdiaconus. Significant hi duo Vetus et Novum Testamentum, sive utriusque prædicatores, quorum lex prior est tempore, dignitate vero posterior.

> Hugo of St. Victor, *De officiis ecclesiasticiis,* II: xiv,
> Migne, CLXXVII: 419.

Turba prophetarum venturi nuntia Christi,
　Mysterium fertur præcinuisse crucis.
Hunc desideriis, hunc laudibus, hunc prece multa
　Præsuspiravit, extulit, expetiit,
Hæc tria commemorat, similique sub ordine ponit
　Introitus missæ, quem chorus ante canit.

Hildebert of Lavardin, *De mysterio, missæ* Migne, CLXXI: 1177.

XII. GERMAN VERNACULAR VERSE[1]

(*a*) The Virgin compared to a vessel of the eucharist.

　　ich bin diu arche in alter ê,
　　lustic geziert: nu merkent mê,
　　dar inne ein guldîn eimer hienc
　　kostpære und himmelbrôt dar inne:
　　dar zuo der bischof selber gienc
　　vürz volc in guotem sinne,
　　dâ Arônes gerte lac,
　　die taveln, der gebote bejac:
　　daz bin ich unde gotes zent.
　　beslozzen in mir din sacrament
　　sint glîch und ouch vil schône verborgen.

Meisterlieder, ed. Bartsch, VI. ll. 200 f. (p. 210).

[1] *Vide* p. 110.

(b) **The Virgin compared to the Grail.**

> Ich bin der siuberlîche Grâl,
> dâ mite der edel Parcivâl
> niect sîn vînde hin zetal,
> sîn wunne lanc breit, sorge smal,
> sîn fride ân ende stête.
>
> *Ib.*, VI, ll. 241 ff. (p. 211).

Wer ledt mich in der liljen tal
dâ mîn amîs kurtois sich tougen în verstal?
ich binz der sal
dar in man daz gespræche nam umbe Êven val.
schône ich daz hal.
seht, lieben seht:
mîn morgenrœte hât erwecket hôhen sanc und rîchen schal,
den niuwen tac der alten naht,
ich binz der grâl
dâ mit der êren künc den leiden übervaht.

> Frauenlob, *Marienleich*, ed. Pfannmüller, XI, ll. 20 ff. (p. 59).

> Du warer godis stamme müter dochter vnd amme,
> du bist der hœst gral!
> dort in dem hemelriche wonstu junffrau lobeliche,
> din wesen ist in got!
>
> *Lieder Muskatblut's*, ed. von Groote, p. 62.

(c) **The lady love compared to the Grail.**

> Diu (geliebte) was sînes herzen grâl.
>
> Ulrich v. Türheim, *Willehalm*, 197. *Cit.* Lexers,
> *Mittelhochd. Hanwörter*, art. *gral.*

> Traut selig weib
> selden sehen überal
> tört mir der synne zal,
> seyd mich zümâl
> deines leibes sal,
> grâl
>   werffen wil zütal.
>
> Oswald v. Wolkenstein, *Die Gedichte*, ed. Weber,
> LXXVI: 2, ll. 1–7. (p. 192).

Ich hör vil sũesser voglein dôn
in meinem haubt erklingen schôn
von oben abher gar zü tal,
das sich mein hertz erwecket.
Gên dir, vil auserbeltes ain,
ich hoff, dû lâst mich nit allain,
seyt dû nû pist mein höchster grâl,
der alles laid verdecket.

Ib., XXXIV: 2, ll. 1–8 (p. 128).

XIII. THE EARTHLY PARADISE, A TYPE OF THE CHURCH [1]

Plantaverat autem Dominus Deus paradisum vuluptatis a principio. Paradisus Ecclesia est; sic enim de illa legitur in Canticis canticorum: *Hortus conclusus soror mea.* (*Cant.* IV: 12.) A principio autem paradisus plantatur, quia Ecclesia catholica a Christo, qui est principium omnium, condita esse cognoscitur. Fluvius de paradiso exiens imaginem portat Christi, de paterno fonte fluentis, qui irrigat Ecclesiam suam verbo predicationis, et dono baptismi.

Isidore of Seville, *In Genesin,* III: 2. *Migne,* LXXXIII: 216.

*De tribus paradisis, et comparatione trium lignorum
quæ sunt in eis*

Tres sunt paradisi. Unum terrestris, cujus incola fuit primus Adam terrenus. Secundus fidelis, quod est Ecclesia sanctorum, quam fundavit et inhabitat secundus Adam cœlestis, id est Christus. Tertius cœlestis, qui est regnum Dei, et vita æterna, et terra viventium, vel potius terra vivens in qua habitat Deus. In primo paradiso lignum vitæ est arbor materialis. In secundo lignum vitæ est humanitas Salvatoris. In tertio lignum vitæ est sapientia Dei, verbum Patris, fons vitæ, et origo boni et hæc est vere vita æterna. Nunc veniamus ad comparationem. Certe lignum vitæ, quod erat in paradiso terrestri, corporalem solummodo vitam sine defectu vegetare potuit. Lignum autem vitæ fidelis

[1] *Vide* p. 114.

paradisi, id est Jesus Christus manducantibus carnem suam, et bibentibus sanguinem suum vitam æternam repromittit, et tamen idem ipse exprimere volens quantum distaret sacramentum a virtute, ait: *Corpus nihil prodest, spiritus est qui vivificat.* (*Joan* VI.) Quasi diceretur: Si me corporaliter in sacramento sumitis, non hoc vobis sufficere credatis, nisi etiam me quemadmodum verbum vitæ sum illuminans animas, justificans peccatores, et mortuos vivificans spiritualiter edere dediceritis.

Hugh of St. Victor, *De arca Noe Morali*, III: xvii.
Migne, CLXXVI: 646.

BIBLIOGRAPHY

This bibliography is necessarily far from exhaustive. It is merely a list of the books which have been most useful in the preparation of this study.

GENERAL

Du Cange: *Glossarium Mediæ et Infimæ Latinitatis.*

The *Catholic Encyclopædia.* (New York, 1907–1914)

Dictionnaire de théologie catholique, Vacant et Mangenot. (Paris, 1909–1913)

The *Encyclopædia of Religion and Ethics,* ed. James Hastings. (New York, 1908–1916)

The *Jewish Encyclopædia.* (New York, 1901–1905)

Patrologiæ Græcæ (Paris, 1854–1866); *Patrologiæ Latinæ* (Paris, 1844–1880), ed. J. B. Migne.

Sacrorum Conciliorum Collectio, ed. J. D. Mansi. (Florence, 1759–1913)

CHAPTER I

Ancren Riwle: tr. and ed. J. Morton. (*Camden Society Publications,* 1853)

Breviarium Romanum.

Cæsarius of Heisterbach: *Dialogus Miraculorum.* (Köln, 1851)

Giuseppe Catalani: *Pontificale Romanum.* (Roma, 1738, 1739)

Catherine of Siena: *Dialogue.* (Tr. and ed. Algar Thorold, with an introductory essay. London, 1896)

H. A. Daniel: *Thesaurus Hymnologicus.* 3 vols. (Leipsic, 1855–1862)

Gulielmus Durandus: *Rationale divinorum officiorum.* (Venetia, 1494)

Nicholas Gihr: *The Holy Sacrifice of the Mass.* (Tr. St. Louis, 1902)

Giraldus Cambrensis: *Opera,* ed. J. S. Brewer (Rolls Series, XXI).

J. Görres: *Die christliche Mystik.* 4 vols. in 5. (Regensburg, 1836–1842)

FERDINAND GREGOROVIUS: *History of the City of Rome in the Middle Ages.* 8 vols. (Tr. Annie Hamilton, London, 1907)

ADOLPH HARNACK: *History of Dogma.* 7 vols. (Tr. Neil Buchanan, Boston, 1898–1902)

EDWIN HATCH: *The Influence of Greek Ideas and Usages upon the Christian Church,* Hibbert Lectures, 1888. (London, 1891)

W. R. INGE: *Christian Mysticism.* (Bampton Lectures, 1889)

Lay Folks' Mass Book. (Ed. T. F. Simmons. Early English Text Society, 1879)

ACHILLE LUCHAIRE: *Innocent III et le quatrième concile de Latran.* (*Revue historique,* 97: 225–263)

ÉMILE MÂLE: *L'art religieux de la fin du moyen âge en France.* (Paris, 1908)

EDMUNDO MARTÈNE: *De antiquiis ecclesiæ ritibus.* (Antwerp, 1763–1764)

F. J. MONE: *Hymni Latini Medii Ævi.* 3 vols. (Freiburg, 1853–1855)

ELSIE CLEWS PARSONS (JOHN MAIN): *Religious Chastity.* (New York, 1913)

BERNARD PICART: *The ceremonies and religious customs of the various nations of the known world.* 7 vols. (English trans. 1733–1739)

DANIEL ROCK: *The Church of our Fathers.* 4 vols. (New edition, London, 1905)

CHARLES ROHAULT DE FLEURY: *La Messe; études archéologiques sur ses monuments continuées par son fils G. Rohault de Fleury.* 8 vols. (Paris, 1883–1889)

DARWELL STONE: *A History of the Holy Eucharist.* 2 vols. (London, 1909)

H. O. TAYLOR: *The Medieval Mind.* 2 vols. (New York, 1914)

THOMAS AQUINAS: *Summa Theologiæ.* (*Opera omnia,* IV–XII. Leonine ed.)

ALGAR THOROLD: *An essay in aid of the better understanding of Catholic mysticism, illustrated from the writings of blessed Angela of Foligno.* (London, 1900)

EVELYN UNDERHILL: *The Mystic Way.* (London, 1913)

MAURICE DE WULF: *History of Medieval Philosophy.* (Tr. P. Coffey, London, 1909)

Chapter II — GRAIL LEGEND

TEXTS

Perceval le Gallois ou *le Conte du Graal,* publiée d'après les manuscrits originaux par Ch. Potvin. (Mons, 1865) This is in six volumes of which the first contains *Perlesvaus.* The others contain the work of Chrestien and his followers.

Peredur the Son of Evrawc. (*Mabinogion,* tr. Lady Charlotte Guest, ed. A. Nutt, London, 1910)

Syr Percyvelle. (Ed. Campion und Holthausen, Heidelberg, 1913)

Parzival: Wolfram von Eschenbach (Ed. Bartsch, 1875); Trans. modern German, W. Hertz (Stuttgart, 1898); Trans. English, *Parzival, A Knightly Epic:* J. L. Weston. 2 vols. (London, 1904)

Diu Crone, ed. Scholl. (1852)

Joseph d'Arimathie; Merlin: Robert de Borron. (Verse, *Le Saint Graal,* ed. F. Michel, 1841)

Joseph, Merlin, Didot-Perceval: Robert de Borron. (Prose, *Le Saint Graal,* ed. E. Hucher, 3 vols., Le Mans, 1874)

Modena-Perceval. (Prose, *The Legend of Sir Perceval,* vol. II, J. L. Weston, London, 1906–1909)

Vulgate Version of the Arthurian Romances. 7 vols. (Ed. H. O. Sommer, Washington, 1908–1913) Vol. I. *Lestoire del Saint Graal (Grand St. Graal).* Vol. II. *Prose Lancelot.* Vol. VI. *Les Aventures ou la Queste del Saint Graal (Queste).*

CRITICISM

Joseph Bédier: *Les légendes épiques.* 4 vols. (Paris, 1908–1913)

A. Birch-Hirschfeld: *Die Sage vom Gral.* (Leipsic, 1877)

E. A. Freeman: *The Cathedral Church of Wells.* (London, 1870)

Wolfgang Golther: *Parzival und der Gral, in deutscher Sage des Mittelalters und der Neuzeit.* (Leipsic, 1913)

Paul Hagen: *Der Gral.* (*Quellen und Forschungen,* LXXXV. 1900)

Richard Heinzel. *Über die französischen Gralromane.* (*Denkschriften der Kaiserlichen Akademie der Wissenschaften,* 40:3, Strassburg, 1892)

W. HERTZ: *Parzival neu bearbeitet. Essay appended.* (Stuttgart, Vienna, 1898)

T. S. HOLMES: *Wells and Glastonbury.* (London, 1908)

L. E. ISELIN: *Der morgenländische Ursprung der Grallegende.* (Halle, 1909)

W. W. NEWELL: *The Legend of the Holy Grail.* (Cambridge and Leipsic, 1902)

W. A. NITZE: *The Old French Grail Romance Perlesvaus.* (Baltimore, 1902)

ALFRED NUTT: *Studies on the Legend of the Holy Grail.* (*Folk Lore Society Publications*, XXIII, London, 1888)

—— *Legends of the Holy Grail.* (*Popular Studies in Mythology, Romance and Folklore*, No. 14. London, 1902)

—— *Celtic Myth and Saga.* (*Folk Lore*, September, 1902)

—— *Recent Grail Literature.* (*Academy*, London, May 7, 1910)

PAULIN PARIS: *Le Saint Graal.* (*Romania*, I: 457 ff.)

ROSE J. PEEBLES: *The Legend of Longinus.* (Baltimore, 1911)

SAN-MARTE (ALBERT SCHULZ): *An essay on the influence of Welsh tradition upon the literature of Germany, France, and Scandinavia.* (English trans. Llandovery, 1841)

WILLY STAERK: *Über den Ursprung der Grallegende, ein Beitrag zur christlichen Mythologie.* (Tübingen, 1903).

THEODOR STERZENBACH: *Ursprung und Entwicklung der Sage vom heiligen Gral.* (Münster, 1908)

F. E. WARREN: *Liturgy and Ritual of the Celtic Church.* (Oxford, 1881)

EDUARD WECHSSLER: *Die Sage vom heiligen Gral.* (Halle, 1908)

JESSIE L. WESTON: *The Legend of Sir Perceval.* 2 vols. (London, 1906-1909)

—— *The Quest of the Holy Grail.* (London, 1913)

CHAPTER III — DIVINE COMEDY

TEXTS

DANTE ALIGHIERI: *Tutte le opere* nuovamente rivedute nel testo da Dr. E. Moore. (Oxford, 1904)

—— *La Divina Commedia*, riveduta nel testo e commentata da Scartazzini. (Fourth Edition, Milano, 1903)

—— *The Divine Comedy*, tr. Henry Johnson. (Yale University Press, 1915.) Passages from the *Divine Comedy* quoted in the text are taken from this translation.

—— *The New Life*, tr. D. G. Rossetti. (1861)

—— *The Banquet*, tr. P. H. Wicksteed. (London, 1909)

CRITICISM

CALDERON DE LA BARCA: *Autos sacramentales*. (*Bibl. de autores españoles*, Madrid, 1848–1896)

E. G. GARDNER: *Dante and the Mystics*. (London, 1913)

ARTURO GRAF: *Miti, leggende e superstitioni del medio evo*. 2 vols. (Torino, 1892–1893)

EDWARD MOORE: *Studies in Dante*. 3 vols. (Oxford, 1896–1903)

J. A. SYMONDS: *The Study of Dante*. (London, 1906)

THOMAS AQUINAS: *Officium de festo Corporis Christi*. (*Opera omnia*, XXIX: 335 ff. Paris, 1876)

KARL VOSSLER: *Die göttliche komödie*. 2 vols. (Heidelberg, 1907–1910)

INDEX

Abelson, J., 104

Agnus Dei, 57, 58

Alberic des Trois Fontaines, 49, 125

St. Aldhelm, 47, 52

Algerus, 56, 81, 89

Allegory, 88, 107–110

Altar stone, 42, 60, 61

St. Ambrose, 16

Ancren Riwle, 24

Angela of Foligno, 25, 42

Anselm of Canterbury, 22

St. Augustine, 16, 19, 74

Baldwin of Canterbury, 62

Banks, M., 50

Bartsch, Karl, 83, 134

Beatrice, 101, 106, 107, 109, 110, 111, 112, 114, 115, 116

Bede, 49, 112

Bédier, J., 44, 53, 54

Berengarius, 15, 16, 17, 18, 21, 75

Bernard of Clairvaux, 21, 110, 111

Birch-Hirschfeld, A., 38

Bleheris, 39

Bohort, 29, 82, 83

Bonaventura, 21, 24, 62, 94

de Borron, Robert, 33, 35, 36, 39, 42–46, 53–56, 61, 62, 65, 66, 68, 74, 78, 123

Brent, C. H., 122

Breviarium Romanum, 24, 91

Brewer, J. S., 52, 71

British church, 47, 50–53, 65, 74, 123, 124

Brown, A. C. L., 39, 122

Cæsarius of Heisterbach, 25, 72, 75, 78, 81, 123

Calderon de la Barca, 98, 111

Calo, Peter, 84

Cantelupe, Thomas, 112

Carmina Burana, 70

Catalani, G., 95, 128, 129

Catherine of Siena, 25, 57, 82, 111, 112

Chalice, 42, 45, 58, 59, 61, 62

Chansons de geste, 54

Chariot, 103, 104

Chastity, 43, 68–74, 79, 113

Ciborium, 28, 55, 58, 59, 60, 62, 63

Conte del Graal, 34, 46

Corpus Christi Day, 17, 18, 93, 101, 102, 104, 105; office for, 23, 94; procession, 94–101, 104, 116, 128 ff.

Cortet, Eugène, 94

Crestien de Troies, 34, 35, 55, 78

Crusades, 39, 61

Daniel, H. A., 116

Dante Alighieri, 11, 12, 41, 87 ff.

Devine, A., 22

Didot, A. F., 36

Didot Percival, 36, 63

Dionysius, 20, 22, 89, 119

Diu Crône, 35, 55

Divine Comedy, 12, 28, 41, 85 ff.

Durandus, 58, 63, 65, 77

Earthly Paradise, 39, 66, 67, 92, 100, 101, 102, 107, 110, 113, 115, 116, 136

Easter sepulchre, 97, 132
Eastern Church, 39 —
Empyrean, 113
Evans, Sebastian, 27, 37, 79

Fécamp, 48, 53, 54, 75
Fertility rites, 32, 40, 66
Fletcher, J. B., 114
Fortescue, Adrian, 109, 133
St. Francis, 114
Frauenlob, 135
Freeman, E. A., 47

Gawain, 64, 67, 73, 77, 79
Geoffrey of Monmouth, 95, 96
Gerbert, 34, 66
Gihr, Nicholas, 105
Gildas, 49, 51
Giraldus Cambrensis, 50, 52, 53, 59, 71, 72, 75, 77, 78, 79, 80, 124
Glastonbury, 40, 42, 43, 44, 48, 49, 50, 52, 53, 72, 77, 125
Gnosis, 4, 19
Godinez, 22
Golther, W., 38, 39
Görres, J., 25, 79
Graf, Arturo, 66, 67
Grail, castle, 27, 66, 67; early history of, 34, 35, 37, 38, 43; food-producing powers of, 32, 33, 55, 81, 123; legend, 28, 29, 31, 33, 41, 44; miracles, 74–82; quest, 31, 32, 37, 38, 42, 44, 83; romances, 33–38; "secret," 43, 53, 63–66; a symbol of transubstantiation, 42, 47, 55; vessel, 41, 54–63
Grand St. Graal, 36, 39, 46, 55, 62, 72, 77, 80, 127
Green, J. R., 14, 48
Gregorovius, Ferdinand, 10, 11

St. Gregory, the Christ of, 25, 78, 79, 114, 127
von Groote, E., 135
Guest, Lady Charlotte, 34

Hagen, Paul, 39
Harnack, Adolf, 13, 14, 17, 18
Hatch, Edwin, 122
Hearn, Thomas, 126
Heinrich von dem Türlin, 35
Heinzel, Richard, 39, 61
Helinandus, 45, 55, 56
Henry II, 40, 43, 48, 49
Hertz, W., 40, 84, 110
High History of the Holy Grail, 37
Hildebert of Lavardin, 16, 22, 23, 25, 64, 70, 75, 105, 126, 134
Hildebrand, 10, 20, 40, 70
Holmes, T. S., 47
Honorius of Autun, 22, 45
St. Hugh of Lincoln, 77
Hugh of St. Victor, 22, 23, 26, 65, 76, 92, 108, 114, 134, 137

Inge, W. R., 4, 21
Innocent III, 9 ff., 58, 70
Introit, 102, 133
Iselin, L. E., 67
Isidor of Seville, 92, 136

St. Jerome, 16, 69
St. John Chrysostom, Liturgy of, 57
John of Glastonbury, 77, 126
John of Ruysbroeck, 25
Joseph of Arimathea, 32, 33, 41, 44, 45, 46, 48, 49, 50, 53, 55, 63, 65, 72, 76, 81, 124, 125
Joseph d'Arimathie, 35, 44, 63, 64
Juliana of Liège, 93

Kennedy, D. J., 84
King Arthur, 47–50, 77, 96, 125, 126
Kiot, 35, 39

Lancelot, 68, 73, 80
Lanfrane, 17, 41, 96, 131
Lateran Council, 9 ff., 58, 64, 92
Lea, Henry, 69
Leclercq, H., 9, 75
Luchaire, Achille, 11, 12, 14
Lydgate, John, 98, 104, 114

Mabillon, 51
Mabinogion, 34
Mâle, Émile, 76, 78, 79
Malory, Sir Thomas, 37, 68, 73
Manessier, 34
Map, Walter, 39, 70
Marie of Oignys, 25
Martène, Edmondo, 95, 98, 133
Merlin, 35, 44, 46
Merlin, Prose, 36
Metrical, Joseph, 35, 44, 53, 55, 62, 63
Modena Perceval, 36
Mone, F. J., 26, 57, 64, 104
Moore, E., 100
Morte Darthur, 37, 66
Morton, J., 24
Muskatblut, 135
Mystic Vision, 3, 22, 25, 42, 66, 83, 85, 88, 89, 104, 106, 112, 113, 114, 115, 116, 127
Mysticism, 3, 4, 5; Scholastic, 4, 21; Neo-Platonic, 4; in eucharistic devotion, 18, 20–28, 42

Naogeorgus (or Kirchmaier), Thomas, 98, 99, 123
Neo-Platonism, 4, 19, 20
Newell, W. W., 39, 45

Nitze, W. A., 39, 121
Nutt, Alfred, 33–35, 36, 37, 39, 61, 74

Origin of Species, 28
Oswald v. Wolkenstein, 135
Oulmont, Charles, 69

Paris, Gaston, 34
Paris, Paulin, 40, 49, 125
Parsons, Elsie Clews ("John Main"), 69
Parzival, 35, 39, 66
Paschasius Radbertus, 15, 17, 76
Paten, 42, 45, 58, 61, 62
Peebles, Rose J., 39, 51, 75, 121, 123
Perceval, 28, 43, 47, 65, 66, 68, 73
Perceval, 36, 44
Peredur, son of Evrawc, 34
Perlesvaus, 27, 32, 37, 40, 43, 55, 64, 66, 67, 68, 73, 75, 77, 78, 79, 81, 96, 124, 127
Petrus Sarnensis, 96
Pfanmüller, Ludwig, 135
Phillips, W. A., 11
Philo, 19
Picart, B., 95, 97
Plecgils, 76
Plotinus, 19
Pohle, J., 18
Potvin, Charles, 37, 40
Prose Lancelot, 42

Queste del St. Graal, 28, 29, 36, 39, 43, 46, 55, 61, 62, 63, 66, 73, 75, 77, 79, 80, 82, 127

Rabanus Maurus, 108
Raphael, 75
Ratramnus, 15
Rawlinson, A. E. J., 122

Rhys, Sir John, 68
Richard de St. Germano, 12, 14
Richer, 125
Ritual theory, 38, 39, 121–125
Rohault de Fleury, Charles, 58, 59, 60, 61, 77
Rossetti, D. G., 115

Sacramental System, 4, 5, 20, 21, 22, 26, 89
San Marte (Albert Schulz), 40, 49, 52, 96, 125
Sauvage, G. M., 15, 16, 17
Scotus, Erigena, 15, 16, 20
Scudder, Vida D., 57
Scully, Vincent, 25
Secreta, 63–65
Shrawley, J. H., 18
Sicardus of Cremona, 57, 64
Sommer, H. O., 39, 46, 72, 73, 127
Sterzenbach, Theodor, 60
Stone, Darwell, 97, 122
Syr Percyvelle, 34
Symonds, J. A., 100

Tabernacle, 55, 62, 63
Taylor, H. O., 109
Tennyson, Alfred, 68, 73, 76
Theodoric, 51
St. Thomas Aquinas, 4, 7, 21, 23, 84, 85, 94, 98, 110, 114
Thorold, Algar, 25, 42, 111, 113
Thurston, Herbert, 69

Transubstantiation, 5, 7, 41, 42, 43, 53, 61, 64, 87; the term, 16, 70; controversy concerning, 15 ff., 65; declared an article of faith, 13, 14; miracles, 43, 75, 83; mystic knowledge of, 21 ff., 42, 66, 82, 83, 87, 88
Trumbull, H. C., 122

Ulrich v. Turheim, 135
Underhill, Evelyn, 22
Urban IV, 93, 94, 95, 106

St. Veronica, 114
Veronica of Binasco, 25
Victorines, 21
Vienne, Council of, 94
Vossler, Karl, 100

Warren, F. E., 51
Warton, Thomas, 52
Wauchier de Denain, 34, 55, 78, 80
Weber, Beda, 135
Weston, Jessie L., 33, 35, 39, 53, 61, 62, 65, 66, 68, 74, 121, 123, 124
Wilkins, 95, 96
William of Malmesbury, 48
Winchelsy, Robert, 112
Wolfram von Eschenbach, 35, 39, 42, 55, 60
de Wulf, Maurice, 4, 21
Wyclif, 15